E-book format

Working Effectively with the

Difficult, Defiant

and

Noncompliant
Student

James D. Sutton, EdD

This publication is published
and distributed by:

Friendly Oaks Publications
PO Box 662
Pleasanton, TX 78064
830-569-3586
830-281-2617 (fax)

Printed and bound in the United States of America

James D. Sutton, EdD
PO Box 672
Pleasanton, TX 78064
830-569-3586
suttonjd@docspeak.com
www.DocSpeak.com
www.itsaboutthem.wordpress.com (blog)

Table of Contents

Epigraph

Teach from the Inside Out

Teach from the inside out on your journey each day.
Sing your own song in your own way.
Awaken, be real, let there be no doubt.
Say "Yes, I can! And yes, I will!"
Teach—from the inside out.

—Elizabeth Jeffries

Author's Acknowledgments: "Teach from the Inside Out" was originally written and published by Elizabeth Jeffries and titled "Lead from the Inside Out." Adapted and originally printed with permission in *101 Ways to Make Your Classroom Special*. It is reprinted here with Elizabeth's permission.

Interventions, strategies and ideas in this publication that are from specific contributors are stated as such. They have provided written permission for them to be shared. Their school, position and grade level is what was furnished to me at the time they contributed their ideas and interventions.

Some interventions, plus a few illustrations, are reprinted from *101 Ways to Make Your Classroom Special*, with the permission of the author and publisher.

PART ONE:

Behavioral Beginnings

Compensate or Correct?

It's generally better to correct a problem than it is to compensate for it. Sometimes, however, the choices are made for us. We don't always have an option.

In other cases, it might be less expensive or less work to compensate rather than correct. In those instances the problem can fester because it is never actually addressed. If the problem *could* be corrected, compensating for it will eventually be more costly in every way possible.

> *You cannot correct a problem and compensate for it at the same time. Compensation and correction are two mutually exclusive, incompatible strategies.*
> **—John Rosemond**
> *Ending the Homework Hassle*

The best cure for a problem, any problem, is SUNLIGHT.
—Anonymous

Example: Lasik surgery is correction; glasses are compensation.

If, for instance, a child experiences the loss of a grandparent, there is no simple correction or restoration of the loss. If we can't restore her loss, we can only help her compensate for it.

Then there are things we could correct, but we choose to compensate instead. Having a slow leak in a tire is an example. Instead of having the tire repaired, some folks might choose to air the tire up every morning. If they have to look for a gas station every morning and take the time to air the tire, what are they losing in the long run?

Dr. Rosemond has a good point, doesn't he? He makes a case for the fact that we sometimes teach responsibility (correction) to a child by actually removing it (compensation). A common example is the way assignment checklists are sometimes used.

Oh the wisdom of that famous author, Anonymous.

A Tale of Two Problems

Inappropriate behavior stems from one of two kinds of problems: inside or outside. If the problem originates inside the student, we can say the behavior is "pushed" out. If the problem originates outside the student, the behavior is "pulled" out. It's important to determine the difference if intervention is to be effective.

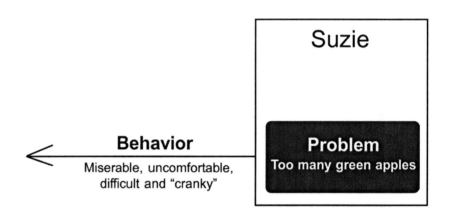

Example #1: Suzie eats a bunch of green apples. Before long she's quite uncomfortable. Suzie's behavior is PUSHED out.

Suzie

← **Behavior**
Miserable, uncomfortable, difficult and "cranky"

Problem
Too many green apples

Example #2: Someone steals Suzie's apples and runs off with them. She takes out after them. "Stop! Those are MY apples," she screams. Here Suzie's behavior is PULLED out.

Suzie

Problem
Apple thief

← **Behavior**
Upset, running, screaming, red in the face, very angry

Into the Classroom

Difficult, defiant and noncompliant behavior within the classroom also follows the "push" or "pull" dynamic. Our effectiveness in implementing correcting or compensating intervention depends in part on recognizing the dynamic of the behavior and addressing the problem behind it, if we can. Doing this requires a knowledge of dispositional versus situational behavior.

Dispositional Behavior (Push): Since the problem is "inside" Suzie, she can have a terrible day when everything else going on in the world is perfect. Fixing the environment at school isn't going to fix Suzie because the source of her misery isn't in the environment; it's inside her.

Dr. Stanley Turecki, author of *The Difficult Child*, describes dispositionally and temperamentally difficult youngsters like this:

> ... *restless and distractible, intense and relentless, unpredictable, uncomfortable with newness and change, moody and overly sensitive ...*

If you have a tool kit for fixing all of that, wonderful. The rest of us will just have to get by the best we can.

This is not to say the environment is not a player in Suzie's behavior; it is. Good teaching won't fix Suzie's apple problem, but a chaotic and disruptive classroom, or aggravating peers, can send her into orbit!

We can't fix Suzie, but we can make the learning environment stable and predictable (where newness and change is not abrupt), or we can introduce her most difficult lesson early in the day, before she gets tired and cranky. This is compensation.

Have you ever seen this addressed in a student's Behavior Plan?

Although it's important that the environment be calm and stable, the characteristics of the environment don't "fix" youngsters who are dispositionally difficult.

It's also possible the dispositionally difficult student can WRECK the environment.

Not exactly the sort of kid you'd take on a three-week camping trip.

Sometimes this is the best we can do.

Situational Behavior (Pull): In this example, Suzie's fine. She's appropriate and resilient but, like all of us, she's affected by situations and circumstances that flow in and out of her life. There are two kids of Situational Behavior: Acute and Chronic.

Acute: This is the child's response to a onetime event—perhaps even a catastrophic event. These youngsters usually recover on their own with patience and understanding. Examples could include the death a loved one, divorce in the family, a fire, auto accident or hospitalization.

Chronic: This is the child's daily response to cicumtances that never go away or show improvement. The cicumstances are not as severe as acute ones but, since they are chronic, the child has no chance to recover from them. An example could be child abuse or alcoholism in the family. But chronic difficulty for the child could also come from a parent who has ongoing unreasonable expectations of the child. This can be a hotbed for defiance.

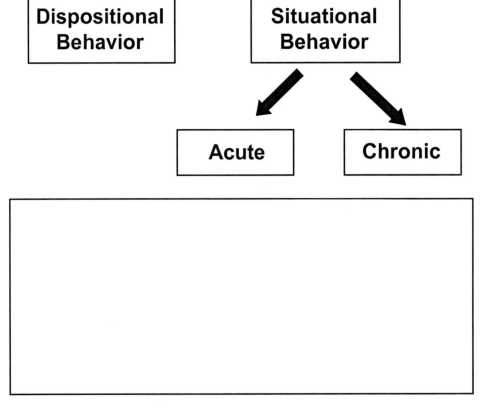

PART TWO:

Getting OUT of the Loop

One way for a person to get folks to do something he wants them to do is to coerce or force them into it. If he has enough clout, enough control over immediate circumstances, and gets angry enough, he can make it happen. But at what expense?

The Loop

Unfortunately, the picture of coercion described here is a fairly common one. It's essentially guaranteed that three things will happen:

1. The compliance gained will be only enough to avoid the full brunt of the negative consequences. Rarely will there be joy or motivation to do well with the task.

2. The person being coerced or forced into compliance will play the "waiting game." The student doesn't have to do ANYTHING until things get hot.

3. The relationship between these two will be either poor or nonexistent. In fact, research shows they make efforts to AVOID each other.

Gerald Patterson, Jeremy Shapiro and others have warned of the self-perpetuating effects of just this kind of power struggle. It's called a "coercive process" or a "coercive loop." In our application these loops pit the adult (teacher or other school figure) against a child (student) with amazingly consistent results.

Coercion is EXTREMELY effective in the short-term, but it's not exactly the way to win friends and influence people—or raise functional children.

Isn't it interesting how a coercive boss always wonders why he spends so much time interviewing for new employees?

It is possible for some individuals to stay locked in a loop like this for a lifetime.

She can keep on doing what she's doing—UNTIL.

Something's seriously wrong when this avoidance becomes a way of life.

Although the results are consistent, the primary players don't always see the problem.

9

A Coercive Loop

Teacher makes request - Student doesn't comply

Teacher "reminds" - Student doesn't comply

Teacher warns of a consequence - Student doesn't comply

Exasperated teacher capitulates

(Student never complied)

OR

Teacher shows consequence ("Crunch Time")

(Student complies "just enough")

Who wins; Who Loses?

There isn't a clear line between winners and losers in a coercive loop, except to say both parties generally lose something. There are, however, some pretty clear facts:

    1. The teacher has more to lose than the student (time loss, lesson unfinished, negativity in the classroom, etc.).

    2. Even if the teacher wins, there will be losses.

    3. The student doesn't have to do ANYTHING until Crunch Time.

    4. With a small amount of "process" the student can dismantle desired, scheduled "outcomes" (Sells).

    5. The student likes this "default" power, and will keep using it (Glasser and Easley).

    6. Neither the teacher nor the student really like the negativity that's generated, but they are caught up in it.

    7. "Take-away Teaching" (consequence-driven compliance) has a short shelf life (Sutton).

One "Cure" for the Loop

One "cure" for a coercive loop is to gain the compliance early in the process so the loop doesn't initiate. (Why on earth would I want a student to believe she ONLY has to do work when I get upset?) Although our best efforts with difficult, defiant and noncompliant students might not be enough sometimes, interventions we will call "Add-to" strategies creatively can encourage early compliance. We'll look at them in Part Eleven.

We ALWAYS have more to lose than the student.

It's interesting how students ALWAYS know exactly when Crunch Time is.

"Process:" Anything a student does deliberately that is not productive to the purpose of the class and takes the teacher off the lesson. (In other words, LOTS of stuff.)

Of the teacher-student conflict, the one who can exercise the most insight and responsibility has to shut down the loop.

"Add-to" strategies won't change the course of education, but they can be productive—and even fun.

11

Soliciting Good Intentions (Neufeld)

Psychologist Dr. Gordon Neufeld suggests that, if a teacher (or parent) has a good relationship with a youngster, an "I need your help" approach might just bring the compliance you need. The "secret" to this approach is the student's acknowledgment and agreement to the request.

Teacher (whispering to student): *Roxie, class will be over in about five minutes. I need for you to stay in your seat until the bell rings. Can I count on you to do that?*

Here's a spin on this same idea; it's called "Time the Teacher." In this approach the teacher enlists the assistance of the problem student, creating compliance through short-term redirection of behavior and focus and, of course, a willingness to help.

Teacher (handing the student a stopwatch): *Jerry, I need your help. I only have ten minutes to teach this next part. Watch the timer and hold up five fingers when I have five minutes left, two for two minutes and one finger when I only have a minute left. Will you help me?*

This is a change, isn't it? Who is usually being timed in the classroom? This approach creates a focal point for all students as they listen to the teacher and watch the fingers of the timekeeper. Important: keep this activity down to ten minutes or less.

Handling Conflict Noncoercively (Kahlman)

In any conflict, the person who can de-escalate the loop and resolve the conflict IS the winner. The diagram on the facing page shows my Sutton adaptation of Kahlman's process for accomplishing this. (Caution: This will not work in all situations.)

Dr. Neufeld is suggesting that youngsters generally intend well, and only need an opening or opportunity for that intention to manifest. (The defiant youngster, however, is not an "average" student. Still, there is much to what Dr. Neufeld is saying.)

If Roxie cares to show she's a person to be counted on, she'll stay in her seat. It's a simple but powerful intervention.

***Helen Jones**, a teacher from Indiana, shared this intervention. We'll look at another application of it in Part Eleven.*

Kahlman's approach does require that the individuals in the conflict have an investment or interest in solving it. (It also doesn't hurt if they basically like each other.)

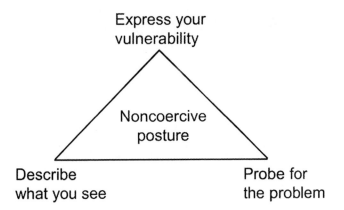

If, in a noncoercive spirit, a person can maintain emotional control while they describe what they see, share what they feel, then ask for feedback (probe for the problem), the conflict is almost guaranteed to lessen. The process continues ("and is there anything else?") until there is resolution. In retail sales they call this "customer service."

> **Teacher (privately to student):** *Tommy, I have noticed that when I give out an assignment, you frown and look upset. I've also noticed that those assignments don't get finished and turned in. It frustrates me when I see a student of mine get further and further behind. What is the problem, Tommy? How can we work this out?*

Classroom Management (Marshall)

Dr. Marvin Marshall's program, ***Discipline Without Stress***, is an excellent example of a classroom management approach that is built on personal responsibility, an interactive sense of community, mutual respect and noncoercive intervention. His web site is www.MarvinMarshall.com.

This process is pretty easy to understand and not difficult to implement. Sell it by suggesting that the person who can implement it really is the "winner."

Have students practice with plenty of role-play.

Keep in mind this process works for adults also. It's a handy tool for managing many uncomfortable situations.

Here's a direct approach that stands an excellent chance of working. Notice the last two questions cannot be answered "yes" or "no." This is important.

This program is excellent. Students love it, also. Check out the web site.

PART THREE:

Patterns and Payoffs

All inappropriate behavior leaves a trail–a pattern containing three elements. All three are necessary for the behavior to happen and keep on happening. If we alter any one of the elements in the pattern, the behavior is altered also. The three elements to a behavior pattern are:

    1. The **BEHAVIOR** itself

    2. The **LOCATION** of the behavior

    3. The **TIME** of the behavior

Behavior

Exactly what is the behavior? Why is it happening? Are there antecedent events, things that come before the behavior and lead it? Do the antecedent events involve anything or anyone that can be changed in a way so that the behavior is not prompted?

*In his great little book, **The Difficult Child**, Dr. Stanley Turecki discusses a Five-day Study Period of a child's behavior (he primarily addresses parents in use of this tool). It is very similar to what you see here: behavior, location and time.*

Location

Does the "where" of the behavior contribute to it? Does the "where" of the behavior set up a circumstance of avoidance or control, a payoff?

It's interesting how youngsters will act a certain way in one place, but not another.

Time

Is there anything important about "when" this behavior happens. Does it only occur when the youngster is frustrated or tired? Does the "when" of the behavior create any sort of payoff?

Want a fourth element? How about People? Youngsters often will behave a certain way with some people, and a different way with others.

Example #1: First-grade student

The teacher instructs the class that, when everyone has put away their art supplies and lines up against the wall, they will go to lunch. This youngster has regular "accidents" at this time, like dropping a few dozen crayons right in the doorway. How might this pattern be stopped?

Example #2: Intermediate-grade student

This youngster eats breakfast at school. As soon as he is finished, he likes to walk around and say "Hello" to classmates by punching them on the arm. They're tired of it. How might this pattern be stopped?

Example #3: Middle/high school student

As class is starting, this student watches the teacher. When she is busy with another student, he leaves the classroom. He walks the halls and the campus. The assistant principal has been dealing with it, but the behavior continues. How might this pattern be stopped?

All three of these examples are real. They were shared with me by educators.

What does it mean when "accidents" become highly predictable?

Why would this youngster "need" to behave in this way?

Like so many students, he's not really a bad kid at all— just socially impoverished.

Recent research has indicated that some inappropriate behavior is "driven." This older student could be an example of it.

Here's a case where addressing only the behavior without considering the cause might mean more aggravation and little change for everyone involved.

PART FOUR:

Defiance and Noncompliance

The "List"

Irritability and frustration

"Forgetting"

Oppositionality

Procrastination

Noncompliance

Obstructionism

Potential versus performance

Arugmentativeness

Provocative and annoying behaviors

What's Missing?

Generally speaking, defiant and noncompliant youngsters KNOW where the line is between annoying behavior and dangerous behavior. Although they have the capacity to drive folks nuts, they don't hurt people. This makes a difference in terms of intervention.

How Serious is SERIOUS?

Per the *Diagnostic and Statistical Manual of Mental Disorders*, the diagnosis of **Oppositional Defiant Disorder** is made when three criteria are met:

    1. Four of the behaviors referenced in the *DSM* are noted, and they have been present for six months or longer.

    2. The behaviors are clinically significant.

    3. The symptoms or behaviors are not part of another, more appropriately diagnosed, condition or disorder.

Intent Makes a BIG Difference

We tend to be tolerant of noncoercive noncompliance without giving it much thought. On the other hand, coercive noncompliance can cause us to lose sleep at night. It's interesting to note just how much difference a little intent makes.

Is Defiant Behavior Ever Too Serious?

It can become so. Whenever a youngster starts adding to his defiance and noncompliance with behaviors that are invasive and harmful to others, he is close to crossing a line. Whenever a youngster repeatedly engages in behaviors that threaten the person and property of others, he has crossed that line and moved into another much more serious diagnostic category called Conduct Disorder.

It's been said that all conduct disordered youngsters are defiant, but not all defiant youngsters are conduct disordered. One key diagnostic clue is the development of genuine and caring relationships. Youngsters who genuinely care about their relationship with the teacher and their peers (and consistently demonstrate that caring) are seldom conduct disordered.

I get lots of email from parents who have diagnosed their children as ODD themselves. This is scary business, as there are other childhood conditions and diagnoses that show similar symptoms. A wrong diagnosis means inappropriate treatment.

"Clinically significant" means the behaviors are harmful to the child's own relationships, progress and sense of future.

If a youngster is doing little work because he is worried about his dog that is sick and at the vet's, we don't see it as willful defiance. This same youngster might even apologize for his lack of focus and effort.

Chances are, if you have a conduct disordered student in your classroom, you'll know it soon enough. (A juvenile probation officer attending a school meeting might just provide a hint or two.)

"Hiding-place" Conditions (Comorbidity)

These conditions and diagnoses (not an exhaustive list at all) can either mask or serve to "excuse" defiant and noncompliant behaviors. It's a way for a student to be defiant and noncompliant and put the blame on the condition.

ADHD, learning disabilities, bipolar disorder, anxiety disorders, depression, diabetes, auditory/visual disabilities, mutism, school phobia (or school avoidance), anemia, asthma, thyroid conditions, tic disorders, leukemia, hypoglycemia, chronic fatigue, sleep disorders, anorexia and emerging personality disorders.

Consider this: These conditions can bring in other professionals (i.e. psychiatrists and psychologists) who might enable a student's defiance with their diagnosis.

What does this mean in terms of working with that child?

Discernment of a student's ability in spite of these conditions or diagnoses can be a tough call to make. Even then, it's very difficult to be certain. We'll discuss this again when we look at confrontation and issues of programming.

Medication: Medication is a big issue today; some folks are for it, some against. A glance at any school nurse's medicine cabinet, however, will confirm that many youngsters are on medications for the conditions on our list and others. Be aware that some medications are being prescribed for children "off label," meaning that, even though the medications might be very effective with some young people, they have yet to be recommended or cleared for specific use with children.

The medication of children and adolescents is a big, big business today.

PART FIVE:

What Works; What Doesn't?

Although defiant and noncompliant students can be different in their behaviors and how those behaviors present, there is consistency in what works and what doesn't work in terms of approaches to intervention.

Which is why we're looking at it. right?

The 2-2-2 Phenomenon

It sometimes comes as a surprise to some folks that not every teacher is having fits with the same defiant and noncompliant student. Some teachers struggle with this youngster while others do not. The "why" of this dramatic difference contains a lot of the solution to working effectively with difficult, defiant and noncompliant students.

This simple observation makes it difficult for a person to put ALL the blame for noncompliance on the student.

It's interesting to watch the numbers. Using an example of six teachers teaching one "difficult" student throughout the day (which likely would be an intermediate, middle or high school student), two teachers are struggling with the student. They are having the sort of ongoing difficulty that is the stuff of early retirement.

Amazingly, these numbers hold up, and are very consistent across the country.

Two of the remaining four teachers are experiencing difficulty mixed with marginal compliance. They're not having as much trouble as the first two, but there's plenty of room for improvement.

Then there's the final group of two teachers who are experiencing more success with this student than the other four combined. It's interesting to note that this phenomenon seems to have little to do with classroom subject matter. It seems to have a great deal to do with differences in the teacher-student interaction. We'll look at this, but first let's look at those factors and interventions that represent what we DON'T want to do with this student—the No-lutions.

In other words, it's possible (perhaps even likely) that this student can be more defiant in an art class than in an English class.

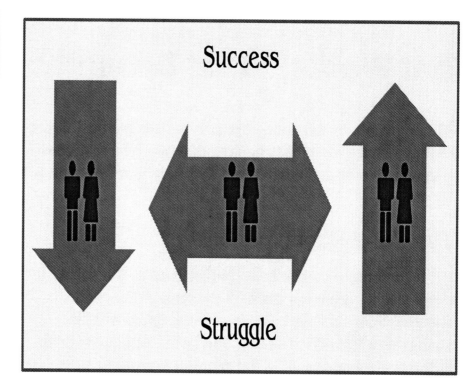

The 2-2-2 Phenomenon

The No-lutions (things that don't work)

The No-lutions aren't solutions; they don't solve anything. We use them because, when we were children, they were used on us (and they sometimes worked), and because we have used them successfully with other youngsters.

The No-lutions don't work very well with the defiant and noncompliant student. In fact, they can sometimes make the situation worse. With the defiant and noncompliant youngster, our first intervention should be obvious: **Stop doing the stuff that's NOT working!**

We will consider seven of the most common No-lutions. Most of us have added to the worn path down this road.

Excessive verbal redirection: If a teacher uses verbal redirection exclusively, it can lose its effectiveness quickly. Additionally, verbal redirection sends the student an engraved invitation to respond verbally, essentially leveling the playing field in their favor. We really don't want that.

We'll later look at nonverbal redirection as one way around this problem.

Coercive response: This could include use of anger, threats or even sarcasm as a redirection strategy. Even nonverbal posturing (a heavy sigh, rolling of the eyes or a pained expression) can be the very thing that sets this kid off.

Example of a response from a student: "What's THAT mean? I ask for a little help—and you do THAT? (While working with youngsters in residential treatment, I got it ALL the time from residents. It's difficult to control when a youngster has pushed you to a point of exasperation.)

Ignoring: Ignoring will not work with any youngster who does not want to be ignored. That student will push their power play until it works.

Pleading: Here's an approach that is highly effective—for about two minutes. Pleading also sends the clear message to the youngster that he has successfully irritated us. Why would we want to give him the satisfaction of receiving that message?

Excessive bargaining: Excesses of this approach can give the student the message that her compliance is for sale and that she can play "Let's Make a Deal" anytime she wants to—and on her terms. We must be very careful about bargaining.

We even need to be careful how and how often we structure choices.

Confrontational help: We offer assistance to help them "understand" what they are to do. The student struggles with us because he understand perfectly; he just doesn't want to do it.

To some kids, H-E-L-P is a bad, bad, bad four-letter word.

Toxic expectations: This redirection is quite tricky because it infers we always know that a youngster CAN do what we ask. This might not always be the case. We'll look at this later.

Expecting a student to do something he CANNOT do is a problem WE create. (It comes close to falling into that category of Toxic Expectations.)

RQ: "Secret" to Success (things that work)

If we could analyze closely those who seem to have the most success with the defiant and noncompliant student, we'll find they have the following characteristics in common (or most of them). RQ stands for *Reasonableness Quotient*; the higher the RQ, the more success with the difficult youngster. The information on these two pages came from observations and interviews with teachers having a special skill or knack for success with difficult students. As you can see, all of these characteristics have the capacity to communicate powerfully when combined with the task strategies we will be covering.

It's interesting to note that Tom Smith, one of the best teachers ever of difficult students, showed us back in the late '30s and early '40s just how much success we *could* have. It's also interesting to note that his most successful students weren't even human.

A teacher with strong RQ (*Reasonableness Quotient*) can:

Separate the student from the problem. This is not always easy to accomplish, especially when the student seems to pick the times and places for defiance that have the most aggravation value. Although it's natural to combine the student and the problem into one, effectiveness of intervention suffers.

Communicate regard effectively. This characteristic is quite powerful yet easy to demonstrate. When a teacher takes advantage of small opportunities for interaction, there is a positive impact. It's especially important that these brief interactions not always be verbal.

Work to avoid embarrassing the student. Youngsters will pick up on this one in a heartbeat.

Pick their battles and conflicts carefully.
Some tolerance is paramount. A teacher who
spends all day hassling with this student will get
little else accomplished. Additionally, who would
be in control of the situation if every interaction
went to conflict?

Make their expectations clear and logical.
This eliminates confusion and misunderstanding
(two tools the defiant and noncompliant youngster
knows how to use well).

Lend empowerment and space. It might
sound a bit strange, but youngsters need an opportunity to exercise the compliance we request.

Remain optimistic regarding change. This is
probably the most important characteristic on the
list. If a teacher loses this one, the others don't
matter for much. (Although we rarely fulfill our
negative prophesies consciously, we often end up
fulfilling them, just the same.)

Project an image of being fair. It's more
difficult for a student to quarrel with the actions of
a teacher who is making an effort to be objective
and fair?

So what should we tolerate?

What should we NOT tolerate?

I once heard it said that young people need two things in ongoing measure: appropriate touch and space. It's interesting, isn't it, that touch and space are on the opposite ends of the same continuum?

We MUST remain optimistic if we are to stay in the business of working effectively with this student.

PART SIX:

Intervention Overview

On the facing page, you will find a listing of all the interventions to be covered in this program.
It is condensed to one page so that you can see, at a glance, the potential interventions possible with the defiant and noncompliant student. If you work with students who are on a Behavior Plan (perhaps as a result of a Functional Behavioral Assessment), this list is helpful.

Here is a graphic representation (of sorts) of a formula for intervention. It is called "Reduce and Raise" because it suggests that intervention involves diminishing some things and increasing others.

The "Reduce and Raise" Formula

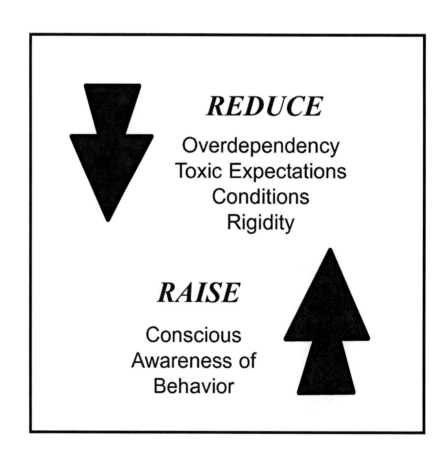

REDUCE
Overdependency
Toxic Expectations
Conditions
Rigidity

RAISE
Conscious
Awareness of
Behavior

Relationship-based Interventions

1. **Expose the benefits of change.**

2. **Plan for some unconditional interaction.**

3. **Recognize appropriate assertiveness and compliance.**

4. **Structure confrontation for maximum gain.**

Task-based Interventions

5. **Present at being reasonable.**

6. **Challenge by predicting subsequent behavior.**

7. **Make compliance an attractive option.**

8. **Eliminate benefits for noncompliance.**

9. **Empower through choice.**

10. **Control for misunderstanding and procrastination.**

11. **Use humor to dissolve blame and redirect to task.**

12. **Encourage and acknowledge self-evaluation.**

Neufeld's "soliciting good intentions" would be an example of exposing the benefits of change.

As we'll learn, this interaction doesn't take a lot of time. 20-30 seconds at a time will do.

If we're going to confront, let's make it count!

Careful with this one. It can easily slip into sarcasm.

This is a big one. There's no need to reinforce defiant behavior.

But not TOO much choice.

Humor can sometimes work wonders.

Part Seven

Change Perception; Change Behavior

We are all fooled by perception on a regular basis. Did you ever walk into a college class on the first day of the semester, take one look at the professor and say to yourself, "He looks like he had nails for breakfast." Chances were, you expected him to act as hateful as he looked.

Okay, so it wasn't your college professor, but how often have you been fooled by a first impression?

But that's where you were fooled. He was actually a kind, gentle man, and he went out of his way to help you and the other students through the course.

And it works the other way, too. Were you ever warned about "the student" you were getting in the fall, only to have little or no trouble with that youngster?

A PLEASANT surprise!

Things are not always what they seem, but we generally expect them to be. As often as not, our behavior changes when we discover that a negative perception proved false. It's the same with difficult students. We cannot affect a lifetime of their experiences, but we can change how they view one experience: their interaction with us. It can make a tremendous difference.

It can make a tremendous difference indeed.

The Kilmer Syndrome

Sometimes students give us mixed messages, just like my daughter's dog, Kilmer. Whenever I played with Kilmer, he was friendly enough. He liked to put his paws on my chest and lick me in the face—while another part of him sprinkled on my slacks. What's the message? Friendly or semi-hostile? The answer is, YES!"

Defiant kids can be just like Kilmer—friendly, smiling and shaking your hand. But watch out; they're STANDING on your FOOT!

Another Four-legged Problem

In all my experiences with defiant youngsters, one observation remains paramount:

As difficult as this student's behavior might be, the child wants you to like him.

Like Kilmer, this youngster sends us two messages, one across the table and one beneath it. It's often difficult for the youngster to verify her difficult side for fear she will lose what she needs on top of the table. This causes us to focus on a lot of problems that aren't *really* the problem (forgetting, poor organization skills, etc.). Nothing gets any better (in fact, it can get worse in a heartbeat), and the problem of defiance and noncompliance moves on from one grade to the next.

I need your affirmation and approval.

I have trouble and conflict with authority.

So how do we work with this youngster when we want to talk to her about potentially uncomfortable things without "losing" her? (HINT: Hang around for Chapter Ten.)

Consider how much tougher intervention would be if all students didn't care if we liked them or not.

The child has a valid fear, a fear of being rejected.

Dealing with all the problems that AREN'T the problem is exhausting!

This graphic depicts what I call a "psycho-behavioral bind." Being honest about why she is defiant (assuming she knows why) might cause a youngster trouble, yet being defiant brings on trouble also. The youngster doesn't see a way out. This is why we have to be careful how we handle confrontation.

The challenge is one of confronting the student without her being afraid of losing our affirmation and approval. It CAN be accomplished.

How They See It

Another characteristic of defiant and noncompliant students is they feel that adults (teachers and parents) always want them to DO something. (They are behind enough in everything that this perception is probably true a great deal of the time.) Still, these students can be reluctant to comply simply because we WANT them to.

Here are three common perceptions underlying defiant and noncompliant behavior. It's interesting to note that these perceptions don't even have to be true for a youngster to believe them and act accordingly.

WHEN Do We Intervene?

There are only two ways to intervene regarding inappropriate behavior. The most typical response (back-end intervention) occurs AFTER the behavior has happened. Although this is sometimes the only option (police don't write you a ticket until AFTER they have caught you speeding), it can also bring on other consequences we might not want.

Front-end intervention is a proactive response; it occurs BEFORE the behavior happens. Front-end intervention often wins over back-end intervention in ways that are quite positive and powerful.

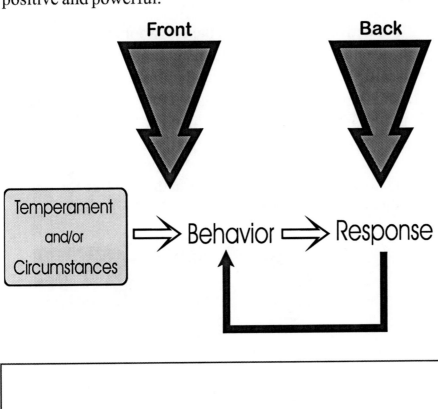

Back-end intervention is loss-related, addresses a behavior that has already occurred, and sometimes requires paperwork (ugh!). None of these are what we want.

With front-end intervention the problem behavior doesn't happen (yeah!) and the student doesn't have to lose anything (consequences). Plus, there's no paperwork or record-keeping.

Front-end intervention, whenever we can accomplish it, will always be more positive.

PART EIGHT:

Reinforcing Relationships

It still amazes me that some folks want to jump right into task intervention with no thought to reinforcing a relationship with a defiant student. To me, it's like painstakingly packing the car for a vacation, but neglecting to put gasoline in it. Regardless of how well the car is packed, it won't go far.

In my opinion, the material in this part of the handbook is the most critical to positive change in the behavior of defiant and noncompliant students. It is no coincidence that the 12-intervention overview back in Part Six started with relationship-based interventions. Relationships are at the starting line of change. Period.

From Aliens to Magnets

Interactive involvement in the classroom is established by the teacher, and it is very much relationship-based. Students will get excited about what they're learning when the teacher is excited about teaching it. True, we're not always at our best EVERY day, but effort and passion about what we do transmits powerfully through the class.

As some time or another, we've ALL had a day like this.

Be honest now. Have you ever had a day like the one in this illustration? Of course; it's part of being human.

It would be interesting to show this cartoon to students and get their feedback.

"WE WERE RIGHT COMMANDER. THERE'S NO VISIBLE SIGN OF ANY LIFE DOWN HERE."

Illustration from *101 Ways to Make Your Classroom Special*. Reprinted with permission

My third-grade teacher gave us an assignment then threw us a challenge. She held up a magnet and a couple of nails. "Will a magnet work under water?" she asked. I could come close to the thoughts of the rest of the class when I say I wasn't sure if it would work under water or not, but my curiosity was on alert. She went on to tell us that, as we finished the assignment, we could, one at a time, take the magnet and nails back to the sink and try it for ourselves—but we couldn't tell anyone what we discovered until everyone had visited the sink. Was I motivated? I would have done just about ANYTHING to have my turn with that magnet. A simple intervention, but powerful (at least for this third grader).

As I recall, it wasn't just the challenge of the magnet and the nails; it was her enthusiasm in presenting the challenge.

To tell you the truth, I would have eaten DIRT to try that magnet.

The enthusiasm of a significant adult makes a DIFFERENCE to a child.

Learn, Learn, Learn—About THEM

We're talking about a little unconditional interaction with the normally defiant and noncompliant student. Although this youngster might have difficulty with this gesture (it messes with her notions of adults), she'll like it.

The secret is to make it specific. Sure, you might know Mary likes ice cream, but did you know that just this past weekend Mary helped her great-grandmother fix ice cream in a churn? Mary handcranked the dessert—and loved it. But you'll never know if you don't ask.

My book, 101 Ways to Make Your Classroom Special (now a best-seller, by the way), contains several excellent surveys and even a letter for collecting this sort of information about a student.

What does Mary like to do in her spare time? Does she have a pet? Any hobbies? Does she collect anything? What are her strengths, her concerns? What would Mary like for you to know, if she could tell you straight out? There are many ways to get this information, either directly or by a simple survey to all the students. You can ask Mary or her folks, or both, but you'll never know if you don't ask.

Relationship-based Interventions

These interventions offer options for individual or group application. At least one focuses on student-to-student interaction. Build on these.

Wonging: This one comes from the master, Harry Wong. He gave me permission to use the term "Wonging." Long before he and his wife wrote *The First Days of School*, Harry made it a practice to greet all of his students at the door to his classroom everyday without fail. He made eye contact and conversation with each of them, often accompanied with a handshake or a hand on the shoulder. Did it make a difference? What do you think?

"H"-Day: The students are told that, as they leave the class, they can receive an "H" of their choice from the teacher. The three choices are a High Five, a Handshake or a Hug. This intervention is so effect students will ask for an "H"-Day if much time goes without one. Once or twice a week is plenty.

Noteworthy: The teacher writes a brief but specific note to every student in the classroom—two or three students at a time. On a two or three week rotation, every student will receive a note, sealed in an envelope with his name on it, on his desk when he walks into class. Each note is unique, positive and uplifting. WARNING: This is powerful stuff!

Illustration from *101 Ways to Make Your Classroom Special*. Reprinted with permission

Pride Tree: The teacher puts a huge tree on one wall, but it's the trunk and branches only—no leaves. The leaves are in a box, cut out from colored construction paper. (Better yet, laminate them and punch them out; they last longer.) As the first few weeks of school begin, the teacher observes the students as they interact with one another and the students from other classes. As she notices a student being especially helpful or kind, she writes what she observed on one side of a leaf and the student's name on the other side. The leaf is taped onto the tree with only the student's name showing. The only person who can look at the back of the leaf is the person whose name is written on it.

This idea grew from a slightly different one shared by Debra Jarvis, a school counselor with Climax-Scotts Public Schools in Climax, Michigan.

The Magic Moment: This is nothing more than extended Wonging, a brief 30-second discussion with a student that focuses completely on the youngster and her interests. It draws its power from the fact the student knows this discussion is not associated with anything she must do—it is completely unconditional. A creative teacher can take 20-30 seconds with a student just about anywhere; it doesn't always have to be in the classroom.

The "magic" of The Magic Moment is not the amount of time spent with the child, but rather the consistency of doing it regularly.

Stick it To 'Em: This is a more structured version of The Magic Moment. The teacher writes each student's name on a single popsicle stick, then places all the sticks into a pocket or a coffee cup. Without the students knowing it, the teacher selects a stick and makes a specific effort to affirm that student in some distinct way. By the end of the day the idea is to have all the popsicle sticks transferred from one pocket or cup to another. Obviously this intervention will need to be lengthened at middle or high school (where a teacher has more students for less time), but it can be done. (And it doesn't have to be popsicle sticks, just something to help keep track of who gets covered during the intervention.)

A great intervention; I regret that I did not get this teacher's name.

Be careful not to drop the sticks!

Sharon Richardson, music teacher at Pomeroy Elementary School in Pasadena ISD (Houston, Texas), shared this intervention.

This idea came from **Nancy Chambers**, teacher at Travis Elementary in Midland, Texas.

Linda Wymar, seventh-grade geography teacher at Vermillion Middle School in Vermillion, South Dakota, shared this idea. The tap dancer is *Cliff Moore*, seventh-grade math teacher at VMS.

A smile and a song: The teacher meets her students on the first day of school with a song ("I've Been Waiting for You," modified from Tom Hunter's song, "We've Been Waiting for You"). Apparently, it has quite an impact as she greets youngsters personally in this manner. She also sings the song to new students coming into her class. In her own words, "No spoken greeting or 'Hello' song has been as effective as this personal greeting."

Read to the teacher: The teacher allows her students to select a book and read to her one-on-one. She says this often becomes more of a sharing time, but that's fine, also. Although it's only a few minutes with each students (while the others are working), it has turned out to be time well spent. She tries to do this with each student twice a week.

Personalized tap dance: Students get their own personal tap dance from the teacher on their birthdays. If he forgets, they remind him. The teacher who shared this idea (not the tap-dancing teacher) noted, "They (the students) love the attention and positive silliness."

Holiday post cards: A teacher took digital pictures of the class holiday party and made them into post cards. Handwritten comments were added to the cards, along with a comment to students about seeing them in the new year. (This was also a great way to thank students for gifts received.) As these were young children, and didn't get much mail, the post cards made a big impression.

*A great idea, huh? It came from **Vonne Walton**. She teaches second grade at Chico Elementary School in Chico, Texas.*

A holiday card: On impulse one season a high school Special Education teacher decided to send holiday cards to her students. She carefully personalized each card with positive comments and dropped them in the mail so they would be delivered after school was out for the holidays.

One of her students died on Christmas Eve as the result of an accidental shooting. Susie and her husband went to the funeral home to attend the visitation. There, on display among the boy's photos and mementos, was her card to him, taped open so everyone could read her comments. He had been so proud of the card he had shared it with his parents.

She now sends out the cards EVERY year.

Susie Rayburn *says she hurriedly picked up a package of Sylvester and Tweety holiday cards and mailed them out. She had no idea, of course, the impact her words to a student would have. It's just proof again of the power of a positive comment—especially when it's in writing. Susie Rayburn is a Special Education teacher from Rensselaer, Indiana.*

The Hug Rug: A teacher took a carpet square and put the words "Hug Rug" on it. Students were told that, when they felt they needed a hug, they could go and stand on the Hug Rug. At the first opportunity the teacher or the paraeducator (teacher's assistant or aide) would go over and give them the hug. Students in class even learned to respond to a classmate standing on the Hug Rug.

*This is a great idea because no words are required, only a move toward the rug. The Hug Rug idea was shared by **Luz Mendez**, Kindergarten paraeducator at Junction Elementary School in Junction, Texas.*

E-Cards: The two hardest things to teach difficult youngsters are anger control and empathy. This intervention is a class exercise in empathy. It requires healthy risk on the part of the teacher and the students. Once or twice a week would be plenty for E-Cards. The teacher simply asks if any student has any worries or concerns they wouldn't mind the class knowing about—in return for their support. As a student shares a worry or concern, the teacher writes the youngster's name and concern on a card, then it is passed around the class. Students can simply write their name, or their name with a comment, or pass it on with no comment at all, but negative comments are not allowed. (The signing can be done as students are working on an assignment.) The teacher collects the cards, signs them also, then gives them to the appropriate students to keep.

> **"E" Card**
> Name:
> Concern:
> _____

Help Me: The teacher asks a student if she would like to help her with something after class, a 10-20 minute task. This would offer more opportunity for interaction. More importantly, it IS a compliance request that is often honored. Just remember it's fine for the youngster to refuse.

Special Time: The teacher sets aside 20 minutes or so after school for one or two days to visit with any student about whatever. Students sign up for this  "appointment," and the time and topic is completely theirs. It's interesting to see how students who often avoid the teacher might relish this opportunity.

Can Thoughts be Replaced?

Although this question might deal more with changing perceptions, something we just considered in Part Seven, I'm putting it here. It is success in relationship-based intervention that makes changes in thought even possible at all.

Dr. Doug Riley, author of *The Defiant Child*, suggests activities in what he terms Thought Replacement. I don't have a handy-dandy format for discussing questions like these, but I would start with small group discussion and try to work it into the lesson. What's important here is not so much what the teacher thinks, but what a student and peers think, and how they express it.

Is being treated fairly important? Do you believe it is a two-way street? Explain.

Just because someone is nice, does that mean they are weak? Explain.

Is it possible to get revenge over something, but lose too much in the process? If so, what should that tell us?

If I said "I don't know" to every question asked of me, what would others begin to think?

What happens to people who seem to never learn from their mistakes?

I can say, "No one can make me do anything I don't want to do," but does that make it really true?

I really like the concept of replacing thought. Since behavior is associated with thought, it makes sense to consider how thought, like perception, can be improved.

I can think of group situations where these would be good icebreakers—especially since there is no right or wrong answer to any of these statements.

It does seem that defiant and noncompliant students are great at responding to these questions—when they can apply them to SOMEONE ELSE.

PART NINE:

Balancing Expectations

The concept of differentiating expectations of young people came from books by Dr. James Sutton and Dr. Ross Greene that were published only a year apart. Both authors suggested that, although it is difficult to get some defiant and noncompliant youngsters to do what we want them to do, putting tasks into some sort of priority seems to help (Greene calls it "Baskets;" Sutton calls it "Balancing"). The premise here is that, if we make everything urgent, nothing gets done. A deliberate hierarchy between categories of tasks lends more empowerment to the youngster, increasing the likelihood of compliance.

High Priority (Basket "A") Expectations are rigid and non-yielding. They require nothing short of complete compliance with no questions asked. Safety issues are an example of High Priority Expectations. Think about this: How many defiant students leave the building during a fire drill at school? Answer: All of them! Evacuation of the building is NOT open to discussion. It is critical to keep High Priority Expectations to as few as necessary. Not every expectation has to be related to safety, but too many expectations placed into this category would put everything back to square one.

Mid Priority (Basket "B") Expectations allow an option of choice. Choice can be structured in such a way that the sort of compliance desired is built into the "menu." CAUTION: Don't overdo choice, else a student will feel she can ALWAYS have a choice or option. This can lead to bigger problems down the road.

Low Priority (Basket "C") Expectations are hardly expectations at all. They are more like "give-backs." They don't matter that much to the adult, but they can matter a great deal to the student. These expectations can even originate with the student. The Low Priority Expectations elevate a teacher's Reasonableness Quotient quickly and help to generate more compliance in the other two categories.

Level of Priority	Interpretation

High Priority (A)

"You WILL do this."

Choice is not an option
Compliance is mandatory
Primary issue: Safety

Mid Priority (B)

"You MAY do this, this or this."

Choice is provided
Compliance is expected
Primary issue: Task completion

Low Priority (C)

"No problem; it's YOUR call."

Choice is allowed
Compliance is inferred
Primary issue: Autonomy

"Balanced" Expectations

High Priority expectations don't have to include safety issues only, but it is important to keep this category as small and uncluttered as possible.

In Part Eleven we'll cover a number of ways to structure forced choice.

Inferring compliance seems to work better with this student than requesting it outright. In this sense it fits very well with Dr. Neufeld's "soliciting good intentions" intervention.

PART TEN:

Constructive Confrontation

Although part of the process of confronting a student is to make them uncomfortable enough to comply, the effectiveness of confrontation suffers if we make the youngster TOO uncomfortable.

Here's an example from history. When British General Henry Clinton took Charleston in the Revolutionary War, he did it with a siege. His artillery could have leveled the whole town, but he clearly preferred a way to win the battle and keep Charleston intact. It's much the same idea with this sort of confrontation of a defiant and noncompliant youngster. We want to win, but we want to keep the student intact.

This approach attempts to affirm and confirm at the same time.

See the programming challenges in Part Thirteen for more information on assessing a student's noncompliance.

The defiant and noncompliant youngster has been confronted thousands of times at home and school. These confrontations are ineffective much of the time because the youngster dislikes confrontation so much he will agree to anything to bring the discussion to an end. Then nothing really changes.

As we considered back in Part Seven, defiant and noncompliant youngsters can be fearful of losing the affirmation and approval of the adult (teacher or parent), so their attempts at "damage control" consist of getting out of the confrontation as quickly as possible.

There's an old saying in mental health treatment: ***If nothing changes—nothing changes***. It certainly applies in our efforts to work more effectively with this particular student.

Confrontation of a defiant and noncompliant student involves dealing with the child's obvious task (and behavioral) resistance while, at the same time, reinforcing the positive aspects of the relationship. In other words, we must maintain our connection to the youngster while we are addressing the problem. The following is a recommended process for a more effective form of confrontation.

Do Your Homework

Exactly what is the nature of the student's noncompliance? Review Part Three and consider the youngster's defiance and noncompliance in terms of behavior, location and time. Consider also if the noncompliance is primarily task-related or behavioral—or both. If you believe the problem is task-related, consider which tasks. Is it possible the student is having difficulty with the work and is just too embarrassed to ask for assistance? Is it a physical concern? I worked with one girl who had such a middle-ear infection she couldn't hear my instructions. That could make a difference. Do your homework.

Confront Privately and Supportively

Obviously, we would confront this youngster privately, unless we want to compound the poor behavior. A supportive, "Will you help me solve a problem?" tone with the youngster establishes the fact that we do need and want the student's assistance with the issue.

Present "Documents" of Noncompliance

Defiant and noncompliant youngsters are the masters of excuses; they could teach us about it! This is why we need to make a case with our evidence of a student's noncompliance. Here are the specific steps:

1. Document a minimum of four episodes of noncompliance.

2. Vary your documentation if you can. Select different kinds of noncompliance, if possible.

3. Present the four episodes to the student in a tangible form (assignment worksheet, a page in the text, a letter to parents that was never returned, etc.), something you and the student can actually look at and touch.

4. Lay these out on the table in front of the student as you express your concern about them. As you finish, lightly touch each paper on the table (exhibits "A," "B," "C" and "D").

5. Pause, but DON'T ask the "Why" question; it won't help. Move to the next phase.

| A | B | C | D |

Draw the students' support; that's a good place to begin.

At least four episodes of the noncompliance should be documented in order to prevent the youngster from trying to make excuses for noncompliance with just one or two specific assignments.

Having the concerns in a tangible form minimizes denial about the noncompliance.

Follow these steps to the letter and you will like the results.

Offer an "Aha" Interpretation

This might sound a bit strange on the surface, but none of us want to hear a "prepared" lecture from an authority figure. We tend to listen better when the discussion seems to be in the moment—spontaneous. Although this is the most in-your-face part of the whole confrontation,  it doesn't have to seem that way to the student, especially if we can get results with the approach.

In this part of the confrontation the teacher, counselor or administrator simply looks at the four documented examples of the noncompliance and offers an interpretation that seems to come to them at that moment. (Although it isn't a spontaneous thought, it's supposed to LOOK like one. And, with a little pausing and searching for a word here and there, it will appear spontaneous to the youngster.)

It's pretty difficult for a youngster to deny her noncompliance when she's looking at four examples of it!

In offering an interpretation of the child's defiance and noncompliance, the adult doing the confrontation offers the student a bit of "wiggle room," so as not to back the youngster too far into the corner. (We want them to help us reach a solution, not become a deer in the headlights.) Here's a "spontaneous" interpretation with three "wiggle room" components marked in bold:

"Wiggle room" keeps the confrontation from becoming so uncomfortable the student shuts down.

> *You know, Becky,* I believe *I see what's happening here.* **Sometimes** it **seems to me** like there's a **part of you** that has difficulty doing what adults in authority are asking you to do.

Stress the parts in bold type.

It is suggested you repeat this statement before going on the next part.

Close the Confrontation

Pause and ask the student if she understands what you said. If she say she does, ask her to repeat it back to you (rarely can she do this). Repeat it until the student can demonstrate the gist of the statement. Pause again, then ask, "Has it EVER been that way for you?" The way this confrontation was set up encourages some sort of affirmative response. Consider the depth of what this means.

Because of how this confrontation was set up, the student would have difficulty denying her defiance.

Even with four examples of noncompliance sitting in front of her, she might answer the question, "Has it EVER been that for you?" with a reference to an earlier grade or another teacher. That's fine.

Follow Up

Let the student know that, if there is a way to silently "signal" noncompliance when you see it happening in the classroom, you would like to us it in order to avoid embarrassing her. "Would you be willing to help me NOT embarrass you?" you might ask.

Wouldn't she have to be extra careful about her answer to this question? We'll look at a specific example of a signal or cue later.

Road Test the Agreement

The first time you employ the agreed upon "signal," make it a role-play situation, not real. This will remove emotion from the intervention, and it will give you an idea if it will work.

It would be helpful to discuss the role-play with the student later. There might be a few kinks to work out.

When This Confrontation DOESN'T Work

There are at least two conditions under which this sort of confrontation and follow-up won't work:

1. The student is too young or too cognitively challenged to understand it fully.

This confrontation has it limits.

2. The student might be conduct disordered, a serious condition we discussed earlier. These youngsters have difficult "connecting" in relationships and in being appropriately interpersonal in their actions.

After all, it is the relationship between the teacher and the student that make this confrontation even possible in the first place.

PART ELEVEN:

Task-directed Compliance

School will always be the most critical environment requiring compliance from a youngster. The cost of noncompliance is failure, retention in grade and a great deal of frustration and concern on the part of all the adults involved.

Although defiant and noncompliant young people aren't likely to be tricked or coddled into compliance, some approaches for improved academic performance are better than others in terms of their effectiveness and their impact on the student-teacher relationship. The strategies and interventions that follow are grouped into nine categories. Each category addresses a slightly different approach to achieving more task-directed compliance.

Failproof Against Misunderstanding

> **Basic premise:** Although this approach doesn't necessarily mean the student will get busy and produce, it eliminates any excuses related to knowledge about and understanding of the task. It's not a bad approach to use with the whole class.

This is an excellent intervention for eliminating any confusion or misunderstanding about assignments and tasks. It does not, however, mean a student will actually DO the work.

"I didn't know ..." insurance: This intervention is a bit of work, so it might not be used for daily work as much as an assignment that will carry more weight in terms of compliance. A paper or a report would be an example. The teacher addresses the class, showing them a card on which is written not only this assignment, but all the specifics of responsibility connected to it (when it's due, where and how to turn it in, etc.). He does not read the content of the card to the class, but rather asks for a volunteer to copy the information onto an easel (flip chart) so the students can read it for themselves. (Note that the easel has a line across it about a quarter of the way from the bottom.)

The teacher deliberately selects the volunteer who, by history, has had difficulty completing and turning in assignment like this one. As she approaches the easel, the teacher whispers to her, "Joanie, read this card carefully. When you're sure you understand the assignment, and you agree to do it, then write it on the board, above the line and large enough and plain enough so every student can read it."

Joanie doesn't have to say a word to agree to do the assignment and write it on the easel for the class to see. She only has to begin writing. That's a nonverbal compliance gesture, isn't it?

As Joanie completes the task, the teacher asks her to explain the assignment to the class and field any questions. The teacher then puts his initials below the line, noting that he is certifying this assignment, which means it is correct and that he can no longer change it in any way—he is accountable to the students for it, and they are accountable to him.

The teacher is accountable for everything in the classroom anyway, isn't he? But making it a statement of accountability makes it seem fair and reasonable—factors that can't hurt the chances for compliance.

The teacher then asks Joanie to be the first student to put her initials below the line with his. Then the whole class, a row at a time, is asked to come up and put their initials on the easel also. The page is torn from the easel and displayed in a conspicuous place until the assignment is due. All the teacher has to do to "remind" them of the assignment is point to it.

Every set of initials below the line provides the nonverbal message, "I understand this and I will do it."

*Thanks to **LeEster Burch**, a second-grade teacher in Pflugerville, Texas, for this idea. She shared that she used this strategy effectively to encourage students to take their spellers home with them.*

This intervention is easily modified to fit any age/grade group.

This intervention came about as a result of an email from a parent in New York. Her 16-year-old daughter was constantly telling Mom the teacher wasn't giving her the assignment worksheets.

Setting it up so she sees the copy of the receipt showing her signature is a great example of the power of a nonverbal message.

I received an email from a teacher who came up with a way to receipt major assignments with ALL her students.

Homework Helper: In this intervention the teacher "reminds" a student of the assignment or responsibility by asking him to help her go over that assignment with the class after the homework is turned in—the Homework Helper. The notion is that, if the youngster knows he will be "on-the-carpet" the next day regarding the assignment, he might just be more likely to do it. ("Assignment Assistant" might be a better title for this job at middle and high school levels.)

Duplicate receipts: Here's a great intervention to use with the student who tells a parent the teacher didn't give her the assignment on any given day. For reasons that will be obvious, this intervention works best when assignments are in a tangible form, such as an assignment worksheet or a written description of the assignment.

The teacher calls the student up to his desk and asks her to bring the assignment sheet. He expresses his concern that she has not been receiving them (as per a telephone conference with the parent), and shows her a new "system" for assuring it will not happen again. ("How can I expect you to do the assignments in here if I'm not giving them to you?) He takes out a "While You Were Out ..." phone message pad, writes the specifics of the assignment on it, and signs it. He then asks her to sign it also, and tears the top copy off and staples it to her sheet. She sees that a copy of the assignment "receipt," with her signature on it, remains in his book. She is fresh out of excuses on that one, plus a little "re-minder" is staring at her as she does the assignment.

Affirm Compliance

Basic premise: It is very easy to affirm noncompliance by giving it too much of our energy. Unfortunately, threats of points off for missing, incomplete or late work don't always produce the results we want. In fact, affirming consequences can lend the student the "default power" discussed in Part Two. The affirmation of compliance is the reverse approach; it's "adding to" rather than taking away. Best of all, it works better with this student.

There will be situations where we must outline consequences of noncompliance with this student. Our emphasis, however, should be on interventions that will produce the best results.

The Great Banana Split Race: This intervention has been around the world a few times over the Internet. Students earn a banana split at the end of each reporting period based on the components of the dessert they have accumulated (spoon, dish, banana, scoops of ice cream, toppings, etc.).

*A big thanks goes out to **Teresa Chambers** for this outstanding idea. When she shared The Great Banana Split Race idea, Teresa was teaching at Sharpe Accelerated Elementary School in Memphis, Tennessee.*

Illustration from *101 Ways to Make Your Classroom Special*. Reprinted with permission.

To avoid any confusion or complaining, each student charts his progress in The Great Banana Split Race. A look at the chart on banana split day quickly verifies what each youngster has earned. The power of this intervention is not in the first time its done, but in the subsequent changes in behavior and performance as a result of past experience. It's the "adding to" principle working perfectly.

Some schools have a policy against food in the classroom. Sometimes this policy can modified, since this intervention is done only once a reporting period. Another option would be to do the ice cream in the cafeteria.

Extra point pop quiz: Even the name of this intervention implies it is an "adding to" approach. There is no penalty—only a way to improve one's grade. The teacher who shared this idea used it in the classroom for 30 years. It's easy to implement.

The teacher makes up a one-question quiz covering the reading assignment or the lesson taught on the previous day. Any student who has been reasonably non-comatose in class would know the answer to the question. Without alerting the class ahead of time (so as not to give the defiant child an opportunity to be inappropriate), the teacher stands at the door and hands out the Extra Point Pop Quiz as students are coming into class. She puts them away after the tardy bell rings. Students are told that this quiz will only help them; if they don't know the answer or get it wrong, they can simply slip the quiz into the trash can. Those who know the answer to the question and earn a "100" are to keep the paper. When a student has five of these, he can bring them up to the teacher's desk. She will staple them together and replace the student's lowest daily grade with a "100." Students learn quickly that a zero daily grade can be wiped completely out if they just pay attention in class, look over the assignments and show up to class on time. (To keep students on their toes, the teacher is careful not to overdo the Extra Point Pop Quiz.)

Pop Quiz Reward: Students who turn their homework in complete and on time can earn an additional Extra Point Pop Quiz. This can help them get the replacement grade of "100" quicker or have a second chance on a missed quiz. Since these quizzes are quick and easy to make up (use a computer template and print them two to a sheet), they make a great classroom performance "booster."

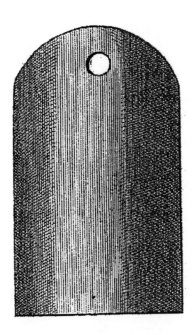

Dog tags: Students who show special achievement or improvement in math, reading or writing are awarded a special dog tag instead of a certificate or trophy. The administrator who shared this idea noted how proud students are to wear these dog tags. (The dog tags I saw had the school's name on them, and noted something like "Excellence in Math.")

Ice 'em down: As a recognition of on-task behavior in class, the teacher gives students cups of ice to crunch on while they work. The cost is minimal, and they seem to enjoy it. And, other than making sure the empty cups make it to the trash can, there's hardly any clean up.

A kernel at a time: Here's a great idea for getting more students involved in classroom lessons and discussions. When a student participates, the teacher gives her a small, paper mint cup. The student dips that small container into a jar of popping corn (or the teacher can hand the student the mint cup already "loaded" with popcorn) and transfers the contents to another container near the end of class. Students contribute to this container all week; it becomes the source for the popcorn they pop and share on Fridays. The message is simple: the more participation, the more fun on Friday.

Ruth Rabago, Assistant Principal at Pomeroy Elementary in Pasadena ISD (Houston, Texas), shared this great idea. Apparently, students of all ages really like the dog tags, also called spirit tags. Sources include School Spirit Products (888-497-7767) or Spirit Line (800-527-4499).

It is my belief that this idea is an especially good way to remember our men and women who daily wear REAL dog tags as they guard our freedom.

This COOL idea came from Kevin Wade, principal of Alexander Elementary School in Commerce, Oklahoma. He shared that the icemaker in the cafeteria made more than enough ice for this intervention—and the cups were donated. (Try to use the softer ice, if you can.)

Kevin Wade, the principal from Oklahoma, also shared the concept of this popcorn intervention.

This intervention might not be possible now, since some schools have policies about food in the classrooms.

49

__Marjorie Clark__, intermediate teacher in Washoe County, Nevada, tells about bringing her Schiperke dog, Frankie, to school with her. Frankie immediately jumped into the lap of her most difficult student. Retrieving her dog, Marjorie whispered to the boy, "I think Frankie likes you best." Thus started quite a friendship, with email back and forth on the class computer. Consider how this student could "earn" another visit from Frankie. Lots of possibilities here.

Homework coupons: Consider partial credit coupons, such as 20-30%. This gives a student a head start and encourages him to do the remainder of the work. Another twist on this idea is to have students come up to the teacher's desk to pick up their assignment, where they also draw a coupon from a fishbowl. Coupons are in low denominations (10-20%), except one or two are for 50%. They do the homework and attach the coupon.

Small denomination homework coupons can also be used as incentives for classroom performance or for turning homework in complete and on time.

Dog-Email: Some youngsters respond better to animals than they do to people. If a student has developed an attachment to an animal that belongs to the teacher (that visits the classroom on occasion) or is at an animal shelter, consider ways that the animal (with some help) can keep an encouraging, compliance-focused dialog going with the student through  email, notes or other forms of communication. It doesn't necessarily have to be a dog, just an animal that means something to the student.

Spit in the Soup

Basic premise: These interventions are provocative; they provoke compliance. Defiant youngsters don't like to have others accurately predict their next behavior. Additionally, they are uncomfortable in those situations and circumstances that cause their defiant behavior to be overly "exposed" (thus they are apt to be compliant, if only briefly).

Spit in the Soup interventions are among my favorites because they tend to fit with my more spontaneous nature. If you're having lunch with a friend, and that friend leans over and spits in your soup, SOMETHING has to happen. In no  way is it an accident. When we use these interventions, and others like them, we are spitting in a youngster's soup.

"Great job:" As the teacher puts the students to an activity, she circulates through the class. Before students have a chance to write much more than their name and heading on their papers, the teacher writes "Great Job!" and her initials on two or three papers. These comments, written on a blank paper, will likely draw some questioning expressions and comments, but few arguments.

Comments like this on a blank paper put the defiant child in a tough spot. If he continues to be defiant, he has to do it in the face of an up-front gift, making himself more of a troublemaker than he really would care to show. Be aware that, on the strength of this intervention alone, any compliance gained could be temporary.

These are wonderful interventions, but not everyone will be 100% comfortable in using them. Just keep in mind that, as you use them, you are affecting the comfort level of the defiant student. That makes it easier, doesn't it?

It might be tough on relationships, but the message could not be clearer!

I was training at Arizona State University when a teacher in the group shared this intervention. I did not get her name. She uses it with great success. It is important to vary the comments written on the papers, and to eventually reach every student.

She also shared that, on occasion, she will put down a number grade on a blank paper (a good one, of course). This gesture has a way of keep the class on their toes.

Eat the chalk: The teacher purchases some peppermint sticks that are about the same color and diameter as pieces of chalk. He then cuts them to shape and scrapes the red off them so they look like pieces of chalk. A few of thee are mixed with the real chalk on the chalk rail of the blackboard, or a stick of "chalk candy" is hidden in a pocket.

During a lesson at the board, when students seem a bit disinterested, the teacher nonchalantly (and somewhat discretely) bites off and eats a piece of "chalk" during the lesson. Chances are, only a few students will catch it, but the word will get around quickly. It won't take long before this teacher will have their FULL attention.

Chalky challenge: The teacher challenges the class that, if they all turn in their papers before the bell rings (or bring the notices back signed by a parent, or have no tardies for the week, or whatever), he will EAT a whole stick of chalk in front of them!

The BIG Picture: This is a great intervention to use with a student who does the same irritating thing everyday, and at the same time and place. To use an example we discussed in Part Three, let's consider the first grader who drops his crayons in front of the door just as everyone is preparing to go to lunch (although just about any example would do).

The teacher intercepts the student BEFORE the crayons hit the floor and initiates a dialog that goes something like this:

Johnny, I want to show you something... (The teacher makes a wide, sweeping gesture toward the ceiling.) *Did you see that?*

No.

It's the BIG SCREEN of my life! (The teacher adjusts imaginary TV controls.) *I'm dialing it in right now, do you see it now?*

No.

Johnny ... it's PRETEND!

I SEE it!

Okay. I'm dialing in yesterday about this time. Oh, look ... there are little things all over the floor in front of the door. Do you know what those are?

Uh ... my crayons?

I think you're right! (She turns off the "TV.") *There ... I turned it off ... but I have a question for you?*

What?

Are we going to have crayons (points to the crayons) *on the floor* (points to the floor) *in front of the door* (points to the door) *TODAY?*

You can just about bet the farm that the kid WON'T do what the teacher has just predicted.

To be honest, this intervention contain some sarcasm from the teacher, but it's not hurtful, nor is it intended to be hurtful. Consider that, if a student has been irritating the whole class with the dropping of the crayons, it would be okay for the class to witness this intervention. After all, the more eyes on the crayons when the question is asked, the better.

I would be inclined to be more direct and private in using this intervention with older students (like the boy in Part Three who kept walking out of class).

One modified strategy for that same older student is the **Colombo Technique***, something the assistant principal might use with an opening question like: "It's really becoming clear to me that you need to get back home for some reason. Is that true?" If the child answers affirmatively, there's something to work on, a specific concern that perhaps can be addressed.*

If the youngster says there is not a problem at home, then the assistant principal could respond with, "Okay, but I'm still not sure. Tell you what; I'll stand outside your class as it starts, and we'll see if I'm right or wrong." It's likely the boy will stay in the classroom.

Please, please be aware that this is only a stopgap measure. If a teacher can continue to redirect the youngster away from the inappropriate pattern, she has a chance to "lose" the behavior over time. Still, it won't address the correcting of deeper reasons and causes of the behavior. That challenge is still very much alive.

Maintain Task-directed Focus

Basic premise: Anyone who has spent a few minutes in a classroom will attest to the fact that there are students who will do ANYTHING to avoid doing academics in class. These interventions focus on the initiation of academic activities, as well as progress toward their completion.

Flat-out trickery: I don't recommend a steady diet of this intervention, but it does send out a clear wake-up call to the student who is always out of his seat doing something useless and time-consuming. My own pet peeve was the kid who wanted to camp out at the pencil sharpener; let's go with that one.

When the class is on task except for the one conducting a love affair with the pencil sharpener, the teacher makes this announcement:

Class, I appreciate the fact you are working so hard. In fact, I appreciate it so much that, for all of you in your seats RIGHT NOW, I have a surprise. (She then gives them something. How about Kevin Wade's cup of ice idea? It has no calories, fat or sugar, and it's non-allergic.)

Is the kid at the pencil sharpener going to be upset? Yep. Will he feel like you have set him up? Absolutely. The teacher processes this BRIEFLY with him:

John, I'll bet you're thinking I tricked you, that I waited for you to be at the pencil sharpener before I recognized the class for being seated. Well, I did. I DID trick you. But here's a promise: Sometime during class tomorrow, I will do this again. John, you're the ONLY student that knows about it.

On the next day the teacher should make a deliberate effort to cut the class in on the deal when Johnny is IN his seat. Message: *I'll keep my word. Tricks are over.*

Random recognition: This interventions spins out of the last one, but with a bit more "distance" for the teacher. Timers are used to catch students working at their desks.

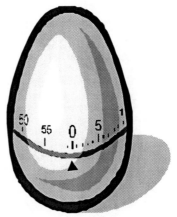

As the teacher puts the class to task, she explains that she is setting two timers. One timer will go off during the first half of the activity; the second one will go off during the last half. The timers are covered in some way, so students can't predict when they will go off.

The teacher explains that, when the first timer goes off, students are to check if they are seated, if they are facing the front of the class and if they have their work materials in front of them. Every student that meets the three criteria can write "FREE" next to one problem or question on the assignment. The student gets credit for it.

Two timers represent an opportunity for two "freebies" on the assignment. Three or even four timers could be used. Compliance is increased, and the only thing given away is an opportunity to make a better grade.

Sticky dots: Instead of having youngsters determine their compliance and mark their "freebies," the teacher asks them instead to raise their hands if they meet the criteria of being seated, facing the front and having all their materials in front of them. The teacher then circulates through the class with some small, colored sticky dots on a sheet, giving one to each hand that is raised. The student puts the sticky dot on the "freebie" problem or question, and gets credit for it.

By "distance" I mean it's the timer and not the teacher that calls the compliance moment.

It's interesting, isn't it, how competitive youngsters can be ... even with a mechanical device.

Notice here the focus is on complying posture only, not what's going on inside a student's head. A student can meet these criteria without actually doing very much on the assignment, but they're not distracting anyone else. That's worth something.

Defiant students don't MIND a better grade; they just don't want to do much for it.

The sticky dots idea is also good for those students who tend to be a little too "generous" with themselves on the three criteria. They do have to get the sticker from the teacher, which causes them to be a bit more objective in their decisions about compliance.

The student can even select the color of their sticky dot.

The Pencil Nap: Here's an idea for getting everyone to stay on task at the same time without interruption. They are promised a break from the activity——a pencil nap (or pen nap).

Illustration from *101 Ways to Make Your Classroom Special*. Reprinted with permission

Students create a small sleeping bag for their pencil (which could be coordinated as an art activity). The sleeping bags are placed on the corner of each desk when this activity is used. The teacher announces that, at some point during the activity, a timer will go off. That will be the cue for each student to let their pencil (or pen) take a little snooze in the sleeping bag (90-120 seconds) while the class and the teacher take a quiet break. When the "Wake 'Em Up" timer goes off, it's back to work.

The Snoozin' Square: Here's the same idea modified for use with older students. Instead of the sleeping bags made by the students, the teacher simply passes out Snoozin' Squares, squares of construction paper that serve as a "bed" for a pen or pencil.

Customized heading stickers: If you fight the battle of incomplete or missing headings on papers, or if you just want to get the students to task a little quicker, consider letting them customize their own heading stickers. That way, the heading is always quick, correct, readable and present. Besides, designing one's own heading sticker (even complete with a little artwork) can be fun.

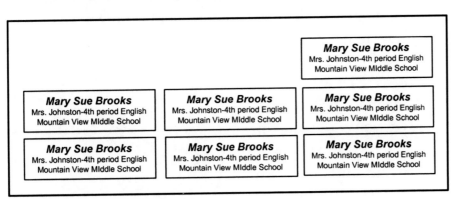

They can be designed on a draw program like Adobe Illustrator, then miniaturized to fit three up on pressure-sensitive address label sheets. Each student slaps on a label, and the heading is done (or most of it)!

If the teacher does all the stickers for the class, they could be managed as address data, easily made into labels. In this way the teacher could put the whole class on one sheet of labels. Each student peels off their label and passes the sheet on.

Time the teacher: This is a great strategy for the teacher who is looking for a short burst of everyone's attention. She hand the most difficult student a stopwatch and asks for their assistance:

I really need to get this part of the lesson taught before the class is over, but I only have 10 minutes—not a second more. Please time me. Let me know when I have five minutes left, then two, then one. Thanks.

Stickers aren't going to rearrange the whole scope of education, but they do serve a purpose, and they're fun.

It is a bit of a chore making your first template, but everything's downhill after that. Suggestion: always convert text to graphics. That way, you can squeeze, stretch and manipulate the text without doing strange things to the fonts.

It's also possible to let students design their own labels by hand using a large format that can be scanned and reduced to any size needed.

The example you see here shows you the possibilities. As you can see, Mary has already used two of the labels.

*Thanks go to **Helen Jones**, a teacher at Cornerstone Behavioral Health in Marion, Indiana, for this "timely" idea.*

This intervention is really a breath of fresh air because who's generally being timed in the classroom—the students, right? Also consider that, if your most difficult student is focused on the stopwatch, he's not as likely to be doing anything inappropriate.

Helen shared that the students really pull her through this timed lesson. If someone creates a distraction, they will take care of it quickly. Like other interventions, it's wise not to use it too often.

Engage Spontaneity and Humor

> **Basic premise:** Nothing defuses difficult situations or difficult people quicker than humor (provided it's not overloaded with sarcasm—something we must be careful about). If we can get a youngster to smile and loosen up a bit, compliance is more likely.

The *Don't Go There* hat: My wife's cousin had an interesting way to let her students know it was time to get busy and NOT come up to her desk. She would put on the most gosh-awful hat you could imagine. The first time I passed by her classroom and saw her wearing the hat, I thought she'd lost her mind—but her students were all seated and working.

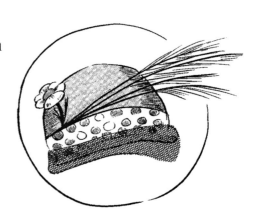

Fly in your homework: The teacher instructs the students to be especially careful to put their name and heading (or heading sticker) on their homework because, when they bring in the homework in the morning, they'll be doing something special with it—a paper airplane contest. Students will fold their homework into paper airplanes, stand behind a line on the floor, and see if they can sail their homework into the Homework Hanger (a large cardboard box placed against the wall). All homework landing in the hanger will earn a 10-point bonus. If the homework lands on the runway, there's a five-point bonus.

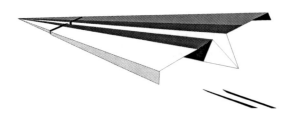

Jumper cables: Here's a terrific intervention to use when the students begin to lose their "charge" by Thursday or Friday afternoon. (You know, that point where the noncompliant kid becomes so lethargic you wonder if he could fog a mirror?) Try the jumper cables idea with the whole class.

The teacher fashions a fake car battery from a cardboard box, complete with a pair of jumper cables. (Suggestion: supersize it and put it on wheels.) When things slow down to a crawl in the classroom, the teacher produces the "battery" and walks up and down the aisles asking if anyone needs a jump-start. (Of course, the teacher lets a student jump-start him also.) After a jump-start, there is the expectation that the student (and teacher) have the "juice" it takes to finish the task.

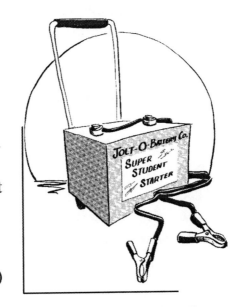

Illustration from *101 Ways to Make Your Classroom Special*. Reprinted with permission

Brain drain: Here's a similar idea that uses an ordinary bathroom plunger that's been sprayed gold and labeled, The Brain Drain. Students request a "brain drain" when their brain is clogged.

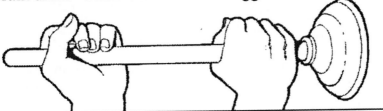

This idea was shared many years ago by a teacher who attended some training I did in Fort Worth, Texas (Region XI Education Service Center). I regret that I never asked her name, as this intervention is a great one.

Experience has shown that young children LOVE this intervention and will participate freely. Older students are a bit more reserved, but they eventually warm up to it.

Brenda Moyer, a teacher at Conrad Weiser Middle School in Robesonia, Pennsylvania, suggests that the "battery" box could contain five-minute jump-start activities to be used in transition time or to reinforce key lesson concepts. Great idea!

This "relieving" idea came from *Martha Lucas*, a teacher at Hunt Elementary in Cuero, Texas.

Another teacher trying this idea shared that one parent was upset that the teacher would use a bathroom plunger on her child. From that point on the Brain Drain stayed on the corner of the teacher's desk, accompanied by a small sign that read: "Self-Service." It was STILL a hit!

Structure Forced Choice

> **Basic premise:** Compliance is a challenge with defiant youngsters, but they seem to do better whenever they can pick the work they are to do. They are more invested into, and more likely to comply with, that which they have selected. It is equally important to note, however, that we cannot and should not make choice an every-time event.

Consider how this intervention employs skills of organization and planning. One teacher shared that her son brings home a packet of assignments for one class. He makes a "big deal" out of spreading them all out on the table and deciding his course for the week. (But he's probably not defiant and noncompliant either.)

Choice of order: The teacher presents the week's assignments to the student or to the class with the stipulation that, as long as they are productive, they can complete the work in any order they choose. (This would have to be modified, of course, if an assignment was built on another.)

Choice of color: As we considered back in Part Nine (Balancing Expectations), it's possible to secure more compliance from a defiant youngster by *inferring* they will do the work than by stressing compliance strongly. Putting assignments on colored paper is one way of accomplishing this.

Make note of the color this youngster selects, and if she always selects that color. There can be a reason for it neurologically, especially if she does substantially better on that color than plain white. Find ways to optimize her performance using this knowledge.

The teacher puts an assignment on several (about six) different colors of paper. (Light pastel colors seem to work best; avoid any colors that are too dark, "hard," or distracting.) As these are handed to the first student in each row, the teacher simply says, "Here's your assignment. Pick a color and pass the rest of them on."

There's just something special about giving school work BACK to the teacher!

Three of five: The notion of a "discard" (blank assignments that can be returned to the teacher) can be a big hit. If the teacher wants a student to do three assignments during the week, she gives him five assignments with the option of returning the two of his choice. He only has to do three of them. (It's possible to "load" this situation by making one or two of the assignments very difficult, thus validating the attractiveness of the discard.)

A "performance" discard: With this intervention the teacher simply offers a "freebie," an additional discard, if all work is completed by a certain day or time. (Set it up to allow for the discard.)

Increase the discard: I've use this one to great advantage. Imagine the student's perception if the discard is larger than the assignments the youngster is asked to do. For instance, the student is asked to do the same three assignments, but she can discard five or eight—or even ten! It's a more difficult strategy to set up, but the impact is something else.

Here's an example of a task "discount" for work completed in a timely fashion.

How could ANY student consider the teacher unreasonable with a deal like this. Notice how this intervention put the teacher's Reasonableness Quotient into the stratosphere!

KEEP   **GIVE BACK**

Build a quiz: The teacher builds a quiz in modules of true/false, multiple choice, short answer, matching and fill-in-the-blank. Students "build" their quiz by selecting the required number of modules of their choice.

The youngster still has to make a passing grade on the quiz; he's just more invested into the process, and will hopefully do better on it.

Combo special: Consider ways to combine the interventions mentioned here. Mix them up and occasionally change them.

There are lots of possibilities here. The student could, for instance, select the assignment AND the color of paper it is on. (Sort of like ordering a hamburger, huh?)

Demonstrate Empathy and Reason

> **Basic premise:** Some youngsters are defiant because they are hurting and are easily embarrassed behaviorally and academically. Efforts of the teacher to recognize and respond to these sensitivities stand an excellent chance of being positively received. A relationship of trust develops. It's no surprise this teacher typically has less difficulty with this student.

Book 'em: It is often the case that Special Education students have reading books and materials that are substantially below age/grade level. To prevent these students from being teased about their books as they move from class to class or travel on the school bus (kids sometimes can be incredibly cruel), the teacher could make grade-level texts and readers available for loan or checkout—just for them to carry.

Something to share: The teacher who presented this simple intervention questioned why we stop "Show and Tell" after the second grade. Although instructional time is a precious commodity in the classroom, an opportunity for a student to share something that's on his mind could well set the table for a better lesson and more compliance. (Premise: If we'll listen to them, they'll listen to us. Even young children understand this.)

Before she starts the lesson for the day, this teacher simply asks, "Does anyone have anything they'd like to share?" To her surprise, a shy student raised his hand and softly said, "My grandpa died last night." Their response to that student's sense of loss turned out to be the most important lesson of the day. But, without an opportunity for him to share, no one would have known.

Capri pants: Now this idea is DIFFERENT, but was apparently very effective. The teacher who shared it taught 17 boys in a self-contained Emotionally/Behaviorally Disabled classroom. Out of her frustration in getting them to attend to academics, she challenged them to a hands-on math project, making a pair of Capri pants—for her. She promised to wear the finished product, no matter what. (Motivation: if they didn't do a good job, their teacher would be embarrassed.) It worked; they got excited and became serious about the project. "They loved the compliments I received and were so pleased that others were proud of their work," the teacher shared.

Renee Pargas, this creative Special Education teacher, teaches in the Ampitheater District of Tucson, Arizona. She told me the boys actually made TWO pair of the pants for her, bead trimming and all.

Hands up: Here's a great intervention for the student who's always afraid to raise her hand in class (for fear her answer will be wrong). The teacher privately tells her to raise her hand with the other students anyway. If her hand is partially closed, it means, "Don't call on me; I'm holding my hand up, but I don't have a clue as to the answer." If her hand is open, it means, "I know the answer to this one; you can call on me."

Karen Westersund supplied this idea. She uses it with reticent students in her class at Del Mar Elementary in Clovis, California.

An "honest" five minutes: The teacher simply requests an "honest" five minutes of work from the student and hands him a timer. The teacher sharing this intervention noted that students are always amazed at just how much work they can do if they decide to get down to it. (I believe also that the word "honest" implies authentic effort on the task.)

This intervention came from *Dianne Herrick* with Ehmke's Childhaven Preschool in Show Low, Arizona.

This intervention fits very well with Dr. Neufeld's notion of "soliciting good intentions."

If the teacher can find out the interests of the students, it's even possible to put photos or small graphics of clip art on the stickers. These can be saved on the computer, and even changed from time to time.

*Thanks go to **Virginia Higgins**, a teacher at Montclair Elementary School in Pensacola, Florida, for this idea.*

This is a somewhat dramatic intervention, whereby some distraction within the square is preferred over the need for constant reminders for compliance from the teacher.

There is legitimate concern that such an obvious intervention as putting a square around a child's desk would, in effect, be showcasing the student's disability. Still, there are those circumstances where this intervention could enable a student to remain in an inclusion class, rather than be served in a more restrictive environment.

Heading sticker gift: Instead of having students design their heading stickers, the teacher could make them for all the students and give them a supply of the customized heading stickers as they move into a new reporting period. Such a gesture deals with improper or missing headings on student papers and ensures that students can get to work on the assignment more easily and more quickly. It's a practical "gift" from the teacher. Everyone wins and, hopefully, more work gets done in class.

Inside the square: The push toward inclusion means that more and more special needs youngsters will be served in the "regular" classroom setting. This could mean more distraction in the case of students with attentional difficulties and hyperactivity. If, for instance, a teacher needed to "remind" a youngster to remain seated over and over again, it could affect the lesson, the class and the student himself.

To relieve these potential difficulties as much as possible, one teacher made this deal with a student. First, she marked out a generous square around the student's desk using masking tape. She then instructed the student that, as long as he remained inside the square, she would not insist he be seated. (I'm assuming here that she situated the student and the square so that any distraction would be minimized.) The student could stand, sit, or even lie down, so long as he remained inside the square. Provided he was not inappropriate verbally, or poke others or throw things, she would not take issue with him, so long as he remained within the confines of the square.

Wipe the slate clean: This intervention came from a teacher's concern that some students carry their mistakes with them for a long time. She saw a need to symbolically help them realize a fresh start, a new opportunity to improve.

During the last five minutes of class on Friday, she encouraged her students to stand and "wipe" themselves clean of the week's problems and negativity. "We would use the motion of wiping our arms, shoulders, legs and shoes to remove things from our slate," she shared. It was also understood that, one their slate was "wiped," students could not again discuss what had been cleaned away.

It's interesting to note that this teacher used this intervention quite successfully—with high school students.

Paper on the wall: A teacher developed this intervention to be used with a specific student. The youngster had a habit of licking his fingers and doing inappropriate things with his hands. His classmates considered his behaviors to be "gross."

In order to keep his hands occupied in a more appropriate fashion, the teacher put butcher paper on the wall next to the student's desk. He was allowed to use his hands to write, draw or mark on the paper, which she changed out as needed. Not only did  his behavior improve considerably, he wrote more using the paper on the wall, adding to his writing skills. The other distractions stopped almost completely.

Veronica Hebard is the creator of this "cleansing" intervention. She teaches math in Morrilton, Arkansas.

*This intervention was shared by **Judith Lister**, fourth-grade teacher at Mause Elementary in Pahrump, Nevada.*

Redirect Nonverbally

Basic premise: Unfortunately with the defiant and noncompliant student, verbal correction or redirection from the teacher can invite unsolicited (and unpleasant) verbal responses from the youngster. This verbal backlash can be of more concern than the original problem. Nonverbal redirection is a viable alternative.

Is it possible that, knowing this student's capacity to turn a small deal into a huge one, a teacher would think twice before redirecting this student at all. Over time, what would be the consequences of that reluctance?

Lori White, *Emotional Disabilities teacher in Knox, Indiana, shared this intervention. She now has several pairs of the goofy glasses, and even lets students wear them when they are doing well and are on-task. "If an administrator walks into my classroom and sees students wearing the glasses, they are thrilled," Lori shared.*

This intervention is a second one shared by **MariLou Anderson**, *Special Education teacher from Grygla, Minnesota.*

"Groucho" glasses: This redirection uses humor, the best way to redirect anyone. It is especially useful if a youngster is not being all that defiant, but is getting frustrated while doing his work.

The teacher quietly slips on a pair of those crazy nose glasses with the mustache and bushy eyebrows, then whispers the student's name. As the student makes eye contact with the teacher, he has to smile a little. This simple gesture from the teacher transmits the message, "I know you're struggling, but hang in there. I'm on *your* side."

Disappearing marks: This intervention shows how a little grace can be more effective than punitive measures. All of this intervention is implemented without the teacher saying a single word to any of the students. That's the power in it.

When a student is not being attentive or is defiant to the point of disruption or distraction of classmates, the teacher writes the student's name on the board. If the student continues in that behavior, the teacher puts a mark by the name, and continues to do so as long as the "problem" continues. If the student appropriately redirects, however, the teacher slowly begins erasing the marks until eventually the name is erased also. Remember, all this is done nonverbally as the lesson is being taught.

The "Good Medicine" Plan: This intervention rewards students for being "sophisticated," meaning that, if a small hint will direct them back to task, there's no need for an unpleasant redirection. This is essentially the meaning of the phrase, "Take your medicine." When used with a whole class, this concept recognizes a level of sophistication. (After all, what student would want to admit they are NOT sophisticated—even though she might not be.) In this case, the "hint" is simple; the teacher silently places a small plastic spoon on the student's desk, which means, "Will you take your medicine?" (Okay, it *actually* means, "Will you turn around in your seat and get busy without me having to do anything more that this?")

This whole intervention can be reinforced by offering it by membership to students who believe they are "sophisticated" enough to handle it. Membership cards, already signed by the teacher, can be used (see the sample below). The advantage to "membership" is that, if a student doesn't take the hint of the spoon (or a teacher has to put a whole pile of them on the student's desk during one period), the teacher can offer to return the membership card and let the student opt out of the "gentle reminder" program. Approached in this manner, the student will often work to stay *in* the program.

*This intervention takes some effort to set up, but it goes smoothly afterward. This is one of a few interventions that has made it around the world several times over as a result of being on the Internet and in the book, **101 Ways to Make Your Classroom Special**.*

Let's be honest; is this intervention going to work with EVERY student? Hardly, but it's worth a try.

After they're signed, the membership cards are kept by the teacher. They represent a contract of sorts. An offer to return the membership card actually puts the responsibility back on the student. If the youngster opts out, she has to be saying, "I guess I'm not sophisticated after all." Since that would be difficult for a student to say to self, she will hopefully give the intervention another chance.

The "Good Medicine" Plan

I think "The 'Good Medicine' Plan" is a good idea. I want to be a part of it.

I. M. Teacher
Teacher's signature

I. Will Doit
Student's signature

Illustration from *101 Ways to Make Your Classroom Special*. Reprinted with permission

Laurie Goodman,
Teacher Support Coordina-
tor from Hanford, California,
provided this intervention.

The most common way the
time is paid back is for the
student to come to the
teacher's class before school,
or stay after school.

Although they are getting
harder and harder to find,
the old-fashioned stopwatchs
works best—the kind that tick
loudly!

Of course, this can turn
into a good-natured contest
of a student getting back to
task BEFORE the teacher
starts the timer.

Cueing: This intervention is much like the plastic spoon on the desk—a reminder. Instead of a spoon, the student works out a signal with the teacher (usually a number) so that, when the teacher casually writes the number on the board, the student knows it is his cue to redirect. This is done instead of a verbal redirection.

Time tab: When the teacher notices a student being off-task or out of his desk, he simply starts a stopwatch or timer and places it on the student's desk. When the student returns to task, he stops the timepiece. It is then the student's responsibility to make arrangements to pay back to the teacher the time that has elapsed on the timer.

The whole idea here is a measure of self-management based on minimal redirection. It is possible that, if this intervention is done with a student who can't handle it emotionally, the results could be problematic (like a timer flying through the air).

Encourage Self-evaluation

Basic premise: When students have the opportunity to evaluate their compliance themselves, there is no one with whom they can argue or disagree. Time and effort spent in creating these opportunities for students can pay off in a big way.

Three-item checklist: Students are given an assignment which has something paper-clipped to the upper right-hand corner—something they can have if they complete the assignment (an age-appropriate sticker, a homework or free-time coupon, etc.). Stapled to the upper left-hand corner of the assignment is a three-item checklist: 1) "I finished this assignment," 2) "I remained in my seat" and 3) "I allowed my classmates to get their work done." All students who can complete the checklist can keep what's paper-clipped to the assignment.

Illustration from *101 Ways to Make Your Classroom Special*. Reprinted with permission.

Work or stand: This is a good intervention to use when a student doesn't respond to the more subtle cues to redirect. On signal from the teacher (or on his own), the student stands and faces the rear of the class where written reminders about getting back to task are posted. The youngster is free to take a seat whenever he decides to comply. The message here is that the student is not to remain seated while noncompliant or off-task.

Earlier we considered an intervention called "random recognition." It also has within it a component of self-evaluation.

It is important to use this intervention sparingly. If done too often, it would lose its effect.

Whatever the teacher clips to the assignment needs to be appropriate to the age and grade of the students. It seems young children like more tangibles; older students like coupons they can cash in for time, activities or an improved or easier grade.

*This intervention was adapted from a more rigorous one shared by **Beth Issacs**, Behavior Solutions Teacher at Marshfield Junior High School, Marshfield, Missouri.*

This is not at all intended to be a punitive gesture. It is intended to get a student to think about what's going on and what he needs to do about it. Frankly, if a student wants to stand through the whole class, that's his choice—so long as he doesn't distract or bother classmates.

This intervention suggests that everyone seated is working!

PART TWELVE:

Gearing Up for Growth

Growth is never complete for the teacher or the student; it's a lifelong process. At best we only have a few years (for many of us it's just one school year—one jam-packed, semi-crazy school year) to create some change in this youngster using some of what has been covered in this program and handbook.

That's a tall order. My guess is, at the end of the school year, we will not be "finished" with this student. In fact, we might still be at the beginning. So? Isn't a solid, meaningful, productive beginning infinitely better than no beginning at all?

My Growth (the teacher)

The process of achieving more compliance in the classroom from this student will not make all his problems go away. (Although I'm very clear on the fact that teachers are not therapists, they are often the best therapist the child has. Think about that!) How we address these questions (after a bit of soul searching) could make a difference on into the future—with this youngster and others.

1. Do I really understand that this youngster's behavior is rarely about me? What does that mean?

2. Does this student see me as a resource or an obstacle?

3. Although I can't change the world for an unhappy child, can I bring a ray or two of sunshine into my part of it?

4. Have I provided the opportunity and the ear to really *listen* to this youngster?

5. What can I do today to become even better at working with students like this one?

The Victory List

The Victory List is an excellent tool for helping youngsters to validate their own success. It can be used with one student, but the effect is multiplied when it's done with the whole group (classroom or counseling group). Have youngsters complete the short list by focusing on just three things they have done well during the week. To keep comments positive, I like to add, "List three things you wouldn't mind your grandmother knowing about." Always structure a little time to let students share and comment on their lists.

My Victory List

1. _____

   _____

2. _____

   _____

3. _____

   _____

What Does it Mean?

First of all, The Victory List helps a student focus on positive, rather than their negative, behaviors. Second, it sets up a great question from the teacher: "Why do you think you're doing better now?" Although a common answer might be, "I don't know," it is hoped the youngster will eventually realize he *doing* some things that actually translate into success. The teacher should gently help youngsters move toward this conclusion, as change requires effort.

The Victory List is actually a redirection in itself, isn't it? Kids can tell you all day how they've messed up, but that's not what this is about. For this reason, youngsters who think they're "bad" might have some trouble with a list that wants only the "good."

Why are there only three items on this list? A defiant student isn't going to give you 33!

The sharing of the lists is an important part of the intervention. Sometimes a student will leave out something on their list that other students remember. This adds to the purpose and effect of the activity.

If students really have difficulty coming up with reasons for their improvement, a question offering two extreme (and perhaps humorous) possibilities might be helpful: "Are you doing better because you are working at it, or are you doing better because the stars in the universe have been lining up just right for you? (Dr. Doug Riley calls the use of two-item questions "splitting the universe." It reduces "I don't know" responses.)

Expressing Appreciation and Gratitude

It is characteristic of difficult, defiant and noncompliant youngsters to become deeply absorbed in themselves and what THEY want. At that point they can be oblivious to the needs of others. They don't care; they want to be on the grand stage and under the lights *all* the time.

Two groups of activities seem to help this youngster take themselves off the stage and out of the spotlight (at least for a little while): activities of appreciation and activities of assistance. Both of these put the focus on the *other* person—a great diversion for the difficult, defiant and noncompliant student. We'll look first at activities (interventions) of appreciation and gratitude, ways for the youngster to say "Thank you" to others and mean it. In my experience, these activities do as much to change behavior in this child as any other single type of intervention.

Exercises in appreciation and gratitude can involved the whole class or a single child. Group work is the best way to start because the expression of gratitude is a worthy action for all to learn. Academics can even be incorporated into these activities.

> ## Gratitude is the memory of the heart.
> —E. A. Robinson, *Captain Craig*

Adopt the custodian: A class could adopt the school custodian for a couple of days or even a week. The idea is to let the custodian know how much he (or she) is appreciated with notes, cards, handmade art, balloons, flowers and plants, fruit, candy, movie tickets and desserts. If possible, give our "target" youngster a central role, such as the writing of the cards or delivery of the goodies.

Flowers for folks: Students decorate inexpensive flower pots and plant a flower in each one of them. These, along with handmade "Thank You" notes, are delivered to homes in the community surrounding the school. The flower pots and notes are, of course, delivered by the students who created them.

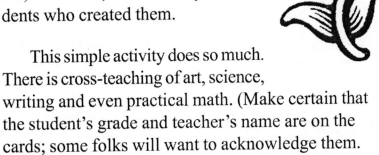

This simple activity does so much. There is cross-teaching of art, science, writing and even practical math. (Make certain that the student's grade and teacher's name are on the cards; some folks will want to acknowledge them. Collect these and share them with the class.)

It's not especially easy to get a shy youngster to knock on the door of a total stranger. Sending students in pairs on the deliveries helps.

This activity encourages healthy risk-taking, and it's a pleasant diversion from the classroom itself. The difficult child tends to "melt" a bit when she encounters the smiles and appreciation of others. In fact, don't be surprised if she really "gets into it." Always process the deliveries later with the class. Students will have stories to tell!

Personal thanks: As a group or individual activity, have youngster think of someone who has helped them the most during the last week or month. Have them acknowledge that person, and share later with the class (or you, if done individually) what they did and how it went. Later, have them do it again, but with a different person.

Different ways: Challenge the class to come up with as many different ways to express gratitude as they can think of. Then encourage them to try them and report back to the class.

Connie Tisch of Jackson Public Schools in Jackson, Michigan, shared this great activity.

Suffice it to be said that there needs to be plenty of adult supervision when the flower pots and notes are delivered.

It's not the intent of this activity to defuse problems, but that is another benefit. Folks who believe students are too loud, or walk on their grass or in their flower beds, might ease up just a bit.

After a couple of deliveries, the shyness shouldn't be a problem anymore.

Don't be surprised if the usually difficult student isn't difficult at all when you get her off school property. The adults receiving the flower pots have no expectations of this youngster, only thanks. Behaviorally, that's a completely different dynamic, and a pleasant one to witness. Process this with the student later.

Wouldn't it be great if students internalized this as a habit? What would others think of them, and what would that mean over a lifetime?

It's always been my experience that the folks receiving someone's thanks get it at a time when they most needed it. Consider the impact of that.

This activity keeps expressions of gratitude "fresh" and unique.

Nurses' station trays: We enjoy holidays and the opportunity to spend some leisure time with friends and family, but hospitals never close. As long as there are people who are sick, there will be nurses and hospital staff around the clock, regardless of weekends and holidays. A special thanks to these folks and their willingness to be on the job, no matter what, would be a very nice and much appreciated gesture.

Consider letting students assemble food and snack trays (complete with "Thank You" cards) that can be delivered to the nurses' stations and the emergency room at the hospital. This gesture is even more appreciated when it is done during special times like Christmas Eve.

Keep in mind that part of our goal here is to get the usually self-invested youngster to focus on others for a change.

Fire station, police departments trays: These folks never take a day off either. They are always there for us; why not be there for them? A creative and heartfelt "Thank You" to firefighters and police officers in the form of food and snack trays would be an excellent activity of appreciation and gratitude.

Offering Assistance and Help

The act of offering assistance to others with no thought of reciprocation transmits one clear message: "This is not about me." That's a good place for us all to be from time to time, but it's an especially good place for a difficult child to visit. Helping others is the quickest way to begin and grow a relationship. Here are some ideas and interventions for getting youngsters started on service to others.

Flowers and bluebird boxes: One school's eight-grade life science classes grow hundreds of tulips in a hothouse. When the tulips bloom they are delivered to senior citizens in nursing homes, retirement communities and private homes. It's apparently quite an undertaking that has the support of civic groups in the community.

These same classes also make a number of nesting boxes for bluebirds. These are delivered to the same folks who received the tulips, and are set up in such a way that the senior citizens can watch a pair bluebirds raise their young.

Banana Christmas: Students often go to nursing homes near Christmas time to sing carols. For the text trip, consider taking bananas, around which students have wrapped red ribbon—a banana candy cane. Give these to the senior citizens in the home. They will be a hit because the bananas are easy to chew (no need for them to go get their teeth) and the potassium is good for them. If you turn this into a banana-eating party, include napkins and sacks for the peels.

Paul Read shared this great suggestion. Paul is a teacher (apparently an eight-grade life science teacher) at Norwich Middle School in Norwich, New York.

Apparently, Paul and his students stay very busy. What's listed here are only two of many projects they take on through the school year. (Paul describes some of them as "self-directed.")

There is a move to put more windows, clocks and calendars in intensive care centers in hospitals. They help reduce the sort of disorientation that can occur with intensive care patients. Perhaps a bluebird box on an intensive care window (in season, of course) would help patients also.

Once, when playing guitar and singing in a nursing home (a volunteer), I saw a group of young people do the Banana Christmas with the residents. It was a BIG hit.

Adopt a senior citizen: While we're discussing senior citizens, here's one more. A class could adopt a senior citizen that lives within walking distance of the school. Having some young people around to do yard work and small chores would be helpful and appreciated. Since school schedules are getting more and more tight, much of this volunteer work probably would be done after school and on Saturdays.

Illustration from *101 Ways to Make Your Classroom Special.* Reprinted with permission.

Emergency backpacks: There will always be students who, through no fault of their own, don't have their school materials with them. It may be due to a family emergency or a child transferring into school on short notice. It could be that a child suddenly had to go to a shelter for their own safety or because a parent was arrested. Whatever the reason, it's embarrassing not to have one's "stuff."

One school started an emergency backpack program whereby students and the community put together backpacks, complete with all necessary school supplies, to be given to students who need them due to emergency circumstances. A small toy is included in the backpacks of young children.

Packaging and stuffing: Students collect and package dog and cat treats to be given to the local animal shelter. (A note inside could identify the class that packaged them.) These treats are then given out to new owners as they adopt a pet from the shelter.

Students also stuff mailers for the shelter.

Adopt a homeless pet: A class makes a commitment to adopt a dog or a cat at the shelter. They not only contribute to the animal's care (until it is adopted), they agree to take turns going out to the shelter and spending a little time with the animal. (Pick a docile animal—a

SPARKY'S CARE IS SPONSORED BY MRS. JOHNSON'S 4th GRADE CLASS AT NEWTON ELEMENTARY

Illustration from *101 Ways to Make Your Classroom Special.* Reprinted with permission.

SMALL one!) Photos of the animal (and even "letters" from him) can be posted in the classroom.

Financing service projects: Students can raise funds for these project though can drives and other efforts, but it's also important to consider the value of letting the community know. They might WANT to help. Also, much-needed supplies can generally be donated. Turn the fundraising into another student project.

Thanks go to **Kathy O'Donnell** for this idea. Kathy is a social skills instructor for the Waco Center for Youth in Waco, Texas.

Kathy also shared other project ideas, but we just couldn't fit them all into this handbook.

It's interesting, isn't it, how a defiant and noncompliant student won't do their math homework, but they'll go out to the shelter and walk the dog.

It shouldn't surprise us; kids often will attach to animals a whole lot quicker and easier than they will attach to other people.

Projects of assistance and help benefit everyone involved. Walking a bit in another person's shoes is good for ANY youngster, especially if the shoes are too small or have holes in them.

Newspapers and radio stations are looking for community interest features like these. These folks can bring a LOT of support to any worthwhile project.

PART THIRTEEN:

Programming and Discipline

Over time, the difficult, defiant and noncompliant youngster presents quite a challenge to us in terms of both programming and discipline. The low-key, but powerful, resistance this youngster puts up creates unusual challenges.

This student is behaviorally not dangerous, so extreme measures on our part are just that—extreme, not practical in light of the issues. Although this child's behavior irritates us and peers, we're more aggravated than assaulted, and more confused than cornered. These youngsters mostly harm themselves, exchanging short-term "victories" for long-term disappointment.

It's difficult to separate programming and discipline issues with this student because the biggest discipline issues are about compliance, and the effective academic programming of this youngster is about compliance also.

Programming Challenges

Programming issues abound with difficult, defiant and noncompliant students. There are at least three questions we must address:

1. **What is the REAL problem?** Back in Part Ten this question was addressed as a prelude to confronting the student. It's always an issue of WILL ("I don't WANT to do it") or SKILL ("I CAN'T do it"), but which one? How can I know—for sure? (The "for sure" part can get fuzzy.)

a ***Will*** Problem "I don't WANT to ..."	OR	a ***Skill*** Problem "I CANT ..."

The fact that these youngsters aren't dangerous is, in a way, a part of the problem. Severe measures of intervention just don't seem appropriate.

Almost always, discipline with this student deals with what he DIDN'T do rather than something he DID do.

Effort spent at digging for answers to these three questions will help you when it comes to intervention.

Does testing indicate that the student has difficulty with some academics? Could this be part of the reason for their noncompliance? Do you see little difficulty in other academics? Or, instead of academics, is the problem more behavioral? Does the child have more difficulty in the afternoon than in the morning (some youngsters, like adults, become more "testy" as they tire)? Does there seem to be any pattern to the defiant and noncompliant behavior in terms of frequency, intensity, duration and course?

Does the student seem lethargic in one class, only to come to life in the next one? Could any of these difficulties be account for by perceivable precipitants not already noted? Does this youngster seem to "target" certain teachers with his behavior, as verified by watching the youngster's interaction with several or all of his teachers.

What about the possibility of physical concerns, like the girl with the middle-ear infection back in Part Ten? Most parents would prefer their child have a physical problem rather than an attitude or behavior problem. That might not be any easier on the child, but it's understandably easier on the parent. (Unfortunately, attempts to address physical concerns or disabilities that AREN'T there only postpones intervention—sometimes indefinitely.)

This is not an exhaustive list, but you get the idea.

2. **Do you have existing programs that "fit" this youngster's needs?** It's doubtful. Oh, there are federal programs, especially Special Education, that are designed to serve youngsters with academic and behavioral deficits, but defiant and noncompliant youngsters don't qualify necessarily. Even if we do

Frequency: How often is the student defiant?

Intensity: How strong is the defiance?

Duration: How long do episodes of defiance last?

Course: Is the defiant behavior steadily getting worse?

All of these are excellent questions. They need to be answered.

It's exhausting me.

They usually don't qualify if the defiance and noncompliance are the only concerns diagnosed.

make this youngster eligible for Special Education services, we quickly discover that he can be as noncompliant with those services as he was before placement—maybe more so. We've moved him into a more restrictive environment, and guess what happened? He brought his problems with him!

3. **What is your policy on retention in grade?** It's possible this student will not do enough work to warrant a move to the next grade, yet it's not unusual that testing will find him to be on or above grade level. In some cases retention puts us in exactly the same spot one year later—with no change. But what are the alternatives, and what would be the "rules" for implementing them.

If a teacher or group of teachers implement the strategies and interventions discussed during the program and in this handbook, it is possible that significant progress can be made with this student within the inclusion (regular education) environment, unless, of course, the youngster is already being served for other handicapping conditions.

Disciplinary Intervention

As mentioned earlier, it is difficult to separate programming and disciplinary issues with the defiant and noncompliant student, as both deal with noncompliance. That will be our focus here, as it is assumed that standard disciplinary policies would be appropriate for other kinds of behavioral infractions.

Two approaches are covered here, one an ongoing school-wide program, the other a onetime intervention with a single student. Although neither of these approaches is a total panacea, they contain a structure that can help bring improvement.

Compliance-based, Zero-hour Programming: Zero hour programming is not a new concept; crowded high school have been using it for years. Using it as a compliance intervention, however, is a fairly novel implementation. By design, it's an intervention that works best in a middle or high-school environment.

Compliance-based, Zero-hour programming is a type of mandatory tutorial with parental support a must. This intervention is implemented on school mornings, a full class period before the first official class of the day. Students are "referred" to the program based on chronic noncompliance in their classes—missing or incomplete school work. They are simply told that they will be in the extra morning class until teachers report acceptable progress.

What makes this program so effective is not what students are told, but rather what they come to on their own. They are having to get up an hour earlier to be at school for this zero-hour class, which means they lose a whole hour of sleep on THEIR time.

After a couple of days students are told they can work their way out of this extra class by bringing in their homework already completed for four days in a row (the number of days can be adjusted). If the student meets the criteria, he's out of this extra class. But he must maintain acceptable compliance, else he is right back in the class again.

As good as the program looks, it can be a headache to implement. There are parent issues (they have to buy into it), transportation issues, logistical and staffing issues. Any one of these can kill the whole program quickly. It is possible to make some modifications to this intervention while keeping the purpose intact. This could help smooth out some of the trouble spots.

Compliance-based, Zero-hour Programming is not something you do on a whim. It requires a lot of preparation. It also requires a strong amount of follow-through until all the problems are worked out.

It sort of hits them like a revelation. You don't need to mention they're giving an hour of THEIR time; let them figure it out for themselves.

It's a simple deal.

Absolutely. It's a program that starts slowly and builds momentum. This is exactly why it is important to commit to doing it for a set period of time before evaluating if it will be continued or not.

The Showdown: This intervention amounts to a showdown of wills with a defiant student. When it works effectively, it's unlikely the student will test the limits again. This intervention is not unique, but the best implementation of it was explained to me by an elementary school principal.

The principal (or vice principal or counselor) encourages teachers to monitor their classes for students who might benefit from this intervention based, of course, on classroom compliance. The principal selects a "candidate" and works it out with the parents that Johnny is going to stay in the principal's office after school to work on homework until it is complete. Whenever it is complete, the administrator will take the student home. The student is not told about this arrangement until school is over for the day.

The principal sits the student down and tells him that he has worked it out with the parents that the boy will do his homework there in the office until he is done with it, then he will be taken home. The principal encourages him not to hurry, that he (the principal) has work to do in the office that will take him to 3:00 or 4:00 in the morning! (The principal is willing to stay all night, if necessary, to get the point across.)

Most students have never stayed up the whole night so, faced with this sort of challenge, they usually comply enough to go home. Just the suggestion of using this intervention again in the future can be a powerful redirection.

This is not a perfect intervention; it has a few holes and concerns. Parents have to come aboard with this intervention to make it work. When they understand that a few hours of inconvenience in assisting with this intervention might make a difference in compliance and progress at school, they usually come around.

There are liability issues, of course, when an adult stays alone with a student after school and in the evening. This needs to be addressed. And, of course, it's best if the adult and the child are the same sex. Staff can switch off on this intervention to reduce the likelihood of any problems.

In some instances the youngster might ENJOY the special attention of having the principal all to himself. In this case, the intervention wouldn't work. In fact, the child might fall back in his work in order to be kept after school. But these scenarios should be fairly rare; most kids put a high value on *their* time.

<u>Do</u>s and <u>Don't</u>s

of the

Showdown

DON'T employ a "get-tough" approach

DO plan and prepare the intervention

DO hold the feet to the fire

DON'T show anger or frustration

DON'T lecture following compliance

There are ways to make it work.

Here's a case where the intervention backfires completely. It would be a time to come up with something else, or put the youngster with a different adult.

Actually, we should do just the opposite—be kind and helpful, but uncompromising.

Make sure you're covered all the way around.

Hang in there. (This student's an expert at cutting "deals" to go home.)

Lectures or expressions of frustration or anger might mean to the student that he got to the adult. Some kids would bask in that kind of control over the emotions of a grown person.

PART FOURTEEN:

Conferencing with Parents

The ability for school and home to communicate effectively when implementing these interventions is critical. If there is any area of miscommunication or disagreement, the child will attack it as the weak spot. And, more than likely, the child will win (which really means she looses).

I've sat in on a few zillion IEP (Individualized Education Plan) meetings; in most of them I wrote the proceedings, the actually documentation that everyone signs off on. I've also provided testimony in hearings that convened simply because the parents and the school could not communicate. No one "wins" these hearings except the attorneys, who often are paid both ways by the school. I am convinced that, in the case of my personal experiences, the hearings could have been avoided except for the rigidity and unreasonableness of just one person. The outcomes could have been dramatically different, and much more positive, with a little attention to a few details in early parent-teacher conferences.

Keep Early Meetings Small

If a first meeting with a parent involves three or more school folks, it should not have been the first meeting. When the school and school district "gang up" on a parent (in the perception of the parent), it will likely send a powerful (sometimes intended) message. But how effective is that if the only thing on that parents mind is getting the heck out of Dodge? They'll sign anything you stick in front of them just to get in their car and go home. Then see if you can get them back again.

Keep early meetings small and as cordial as possible.

Greet Them Warmly

For some parents the act of coming to the school for a conference involves sacrifice. They might have to take off work and lose pay, they might have to arrange child care and even beg or borrow a ride to the school. Let them know you appreciate them being there, and the effort it involved. Offer them some simple refreshments.

Consider, too, that some parents might not have had good experiences in school themselves. Even coming to the conference might be quite an uncomfortable visit for them.

Be prepared if a parent must bring small children with them. Have a few toys on hand. Rapport-building small talk is fine, but if a parent is obviously nervous, I'd get down to business fairly quickly.

Make very certain they are SOFT toys. That way, if they go flying around the room, no one gets clobbered.

Give Them a "Friendly Folder"

One teacher greats parents then, as they sit down to conference, she hand them a manila folder that looks *exactly* like the one she has. It's a gesture that's simple, warm—and brilliant. (What do parents generally bring with them to a conference? Nothing, right?) The folder levels the playing field, saying to the parent, "You're a full partner in what we do here." That has impact.

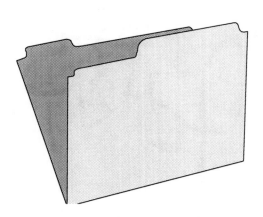

I've come to call this folder the "Friendly Folder." It contains a pen or pencil, something for taking notes, a copy of the school calendar, samples of the child's work and discipline referrals, if any.

*This has to be one of the greatest single ideas I've ever received. It was shared at a workshop (sponsored by Indiana University) by **Lori Houston**, school psychologist with Johnson County Schools in Indiana.*

My last year in the public schools, I did the cumulative writing, the proceedings, of 223 IEP meetings. I *never* offered a "Friendly Folder." (I did provide federally mandated documentation, which I'm convinced scared the liver out of some parents—it would me.) If and when I'm in that situation again, I'm doing the "Friendly Folder."

Yes, 223. I think they settled in my bones.

Don't Overwhelm Them

The mind effectively can handle new information in small "bites." Too much, and most of it is lost. It's better to have another meeting with the parent than to attempt to cover too much in one sitting.

Be aware of physically overwhelming the parent. It's a subtle thing, but it's often there. I've walked into meetings that had school folks on one side of the table and the parent, alone, on the other. It looked more like a deposition than a meeting. It's not a great way to draw the support and help of a key player in the desired academic and behavioral improvement of the student.

Outline the Bigger Picture

Parents can't possibly know what we fail to tell them. If we're worried about the ulti- mate effects of chronic noncom- pliance (failure in grade and possi- bly failure to graduate—even difficulty with future employ- ment), we're not communicating. This parent

might truly be confused and wonder what all the "flap" is about—unless we tell them clearly. Let them know the "costs" of doing little or nothing and exactly why an imme- diate course of action is necessary.

Note That Change Will be Uncomfortable

Change takes us all out of our comfort zones. It's been said that we change ONLY when the fear of the consequences of not changing outweigh the effort to change. Although this applies to everyone who is maintaining operational body temperature, it absolutely applies to the difficult, defiant and noncompliant child.

Think about it. If this youngster KNEW what she could do that would make her life more livable and pleasant, wouldn't she have done it a long time ago? I'm clear on the fact this youngster doesn't like the grief her behavior brings her, but she's "comfortable" with it. After all, she's getting a steady stream of small (and sometimes not-so-small) payoffs from it. Consider this meeting, for instance. You don't think this child's aware that, although she never gets five minutes of interaction with her mother or father, she can engage in behaviors at school that force both Mom and Dad into long and often difficult meetings at school? And we're going to ask her to give that up?

If we can get some change going with the student, it might mean that she is more direct and honest in telling us what the problem is (from her perspective), instead of being noncompliant and just not doing it. (Listen, if I can get a youngster to TALK to me, I've got a chance of working out the problem.) That's improvement.

But it might look like anything BUT improvement to a parent. It might look like a kid who's become brazen and sassy. Now, instead of not eating everything on her plate, or not feeding the dog, the daughter complains about the mashed potatoes or that it's unfair that she should be the only one having to feed the dog. If they're not careful, instead of working out the problem (making the potatoes a different way when she promises to try them, or trading out chores with other siblings), the parents will punish the honesty. Then things go right back to how they used to be.

Let the folks know change WILL be uncomfortable, but that's the price of progress.

In the long-run, isn't this why a defiant youngster would stop being defiant? If so, then our responsibility is to make the effort required to change as achievable as we can.

I've visited with a lot of youngsters as a psychologist. I'm convinced that just about all of them knew when they were unhappy, but few of them really had much of a clue as to what they could do to BE happy. They think they know, but they're usually wrong. Adults aren't much different.

Parents really need to see this as improvement over the way things were.

A little discomfort sometimes can be a good thing. It says we're getting out of our comfort zones and doing something daring and different.

Have Action Items for Everyone

If this conference is about making changes and implementing intervention, then EVERY person in the meeting should have an investment in the process, some actionable gesture of connection and accountability. Too often it's been my experience that, during these conferences, the school makes all the commitments while the parent makes none. Everyone, including the parent, should have something for which they are accountable as a result of this meeting.

I worked once with a situation that involved a head-strong sophomore girl. She showed up late for her first class every Monday morning. She was pretty good about making her other classes on time, but there was something about Monday morning; she was *always* late. In a school conference the girl's mother was asked to be certain her daughter was in class on time for first period, but only on Mondays. That was a commitment, but not an overwhelming request. The Monday morning problem stopped after that.

Set a Time for the Next Meeting

This might be the most important part of the whole conference, the setting of a time to meet again to see how the intervention plan is going and how it can be improved.

The advantage of setting this meeting at the closing of the first is that it establishes everyone's accountability to do whatever it is they have agreed to do—their action or intervention. They not only know they will be accountable, they know when they will be required to explain their involvement to the group.

Also, if another meeting is set, there will hopefully be some good things to report. But if we call the meeting later, it could be all problem-generated. We don't want that.

How can the parent feel a part of the conference if we don't give them a "job" to do with the child also?

This was a perfect "job" for the parent. It not only dealt with the tardiness problems on Mondays, it make the parent a full and complete player in the school success of her daughter. Everyone was a winner.

I'm not talking about IEP review meetings here. They are set by federal guidelines. Special Education folks stay busy enough without doubling up on required meetings.

If the first meeting was productive, there WILL be some good things to report.

PART FIFTEEN:

What We've Covered Here

We've covered a lot of material in a fairly short period of time. As a quick review, you will note we have covered the following:

1. The difference between compensating versus correcting issues relating to compliance

2. How inappropriate behavior is caused by "push" or "pull" problems

3. A look at dispositional versus situational behaviors in the classroom

4. How situational behavior can be acute or chronic in origin

5. Coercive loops in teacher-student interaction

6. A model of a coercive loop

7. Seven ways a coercive loop can be costly in the classroom

8. One cure for a coercive loop

9. Neufeld's concept of "soliciting good intentions"

10. How to teach students to handle anger and conflict noncoercively

11. The noncoercive characteristics of Marshall's *Discipline without Stress* approach to classroom management

12. Three elements to a behavior pattern and how to handle them

13. Practice in the brainstorming of ways to alter behavior patterns using examples of three specific age-grade groups

14. Nine types of defiant and noncompliant behavior

15. How defiant behavior can become *Oppositional Defiant Disorder*

16. Conditions and diagnoses that provide a convenient "hiding place" for defiance and noncompliance

17. The *2-2-2 Phenomenon*—the fact there are adults who have LITTLE difficulty with this student

18. *No-lutions*—seven things we do sometimes that DON'T WORK!

19. Eight characteristics of teachers who successfully realize compliance with this student (the *Reasonableness Quotient*)

20. A 12-part overview of relationship and task-based interventions

21. A model for the *"Reduce and Raise" Formula*

22. How altering a student's perception can change behavior

23. Practice in ways to create changes in three critical perceptions

24. The value of the "when" of intervention

25. How relationships are positioned at the starting line of change

26. 15 specific relationship-based interventions

27. Riley's thoughts on thought replacement—another adjunct to intervention

28. How balancing expectations can achieve compliance on high-priority tasks

29. The *"Balanced" Expectations* model

30. A process for constructively and effectively confronting this student's defiance and noncompliance

31. Three interventions for preventing the misunderstanding of directions and tasks

32. Eight interventions for achieving compliance by "adding to" rather than taking away

33. Four fun and creative "Spit-in-the-Soup" interventions for gaining cooperation and compliance

Part Sixteen:

References

American Psychiatric Association, *Diagnostic and statistical manual of mental disorders IV* (Text Revision). Washington, D.C.: APA, 2000

Barkley, R., *Defiant children: a clinician's manual for parent training.* New York: Guilford Press, 1987.

Barkley, R., Benton, C., *Your defiant child.* New York: Guilford Press, 1998.

Bernstein, J., *10 days to a less defiant child.* New York, NY: Marlowe & Company, 2006.

Biederman, J., Newcorn, J., Sprich, S., "Comorbidity of attention deficit hyperactivity disorder with conduct, depressive, anxiety, and other disorders." *American Journal of Psychiatry* 1991; 148:564-577.

Biederman, J., Faraone, S., Milberger, S., Jetton, J., Chen, L., Mick, E., Greene, R., Russell, R., "Is childhood oppositional defiant disorder a precursor to adolescent conduct disorder? Findings from a four-year follow-up study of children with ADHD." *Journal of the American Academy of Child and Adolescent Psychiatry* 1996, 34(9): 1193-1204.

Bodenhamer, G., *Back in control: how to get your children to behave.* New York: Simon & Schuster (Fireside edition), 1992.

Cantwell, D., Baker, L., "Stability and natural history of DSM-III childhood disgnoses." *Journal of the American Academy of Child and Adolescent Psychiatry* 1989; 28;691-700.

Cummins, K., *The teacher's guide to behavioral interventions: intervention strategies for behavior problems in the educational environment.* Columbia, MO: Hawthorne Educational Services, 1988.

Glasser, H., Easley, J., *Transforming the difficult child: the nurtured heart approach.* Tucson, AZ: Glasser & Easley, 1999.

Greene, R., *The explosive child*. New York: HarperCollins, 1998.

Greene, R., *Explosive/noncompliant children and adolescents*. A workshop presented for the New England Educational Institute in San Antonio, Texas: October, 1999.

Hancock, L., "Mother's little helper." *Newsweek*; March 18, 1996; 51-55.

Kashani, J., Beck, N., Hoeper, E., Reid, J., "Psychiatric disorders in a community sample of adolescents." American Journal of Psychiatry 1987; 144:584-589; correction 144:1114.

Long, N., Long, J., *The angry smile: managing passive aggressive behavior*. Austin, TX: Pro-Ed, 2001.

Marshall, M., *Discipline without stress, punishments or rewards*. Las Alamitas, CA: Piper Press, 2001.

McMahon, R., Forehand, R., "Parent training for the noncompliant child: treatment outcome, generalization, and adjunctive therapy procedures," in *Parent training: foundations of research and practice*. Edited by Dangle, R., Polster, R., New York: Guilford Press, 1984; 298-328.

Morrison, E., "Underachievement among preadolescent boys considered in relation to passive aggression." *Journal of Educational Psychology* 1969, 60 (3) 168-173.

Neufeld, G., Mate, G., *Hold on to your kids: why parents need to matter more than peers*. New York, NY: Ballantine Books, 2005.

Patterson, G., *Coercive family process* (social learning approach, vol 3). Eugene, OR: Castalia Publishing Company, 1982.

Pelham, W., "Teacher ratings of DSM III-R symptoms for the disruptive disorders." *Journal of the American Academy of Child and Adolescent Psychiatry* 1992; 31:210-218.

Rey, J., "Oppositional defiant disorder." *American Journal of Psychiatry* 1993; 150(12):1769-1778.

Rey, J., Bashir, M., Schwarz, M., Richards, I., Plapp, J., Stewart, G., "Oppositional disorder; fact or fiction?" *Journal of the American Academy of Child and Adolescent Psychiatry* 1988; 27:157-162.

Riley, D., *The defiant child: a parent's guide to oppositional defiant disorder.* Dallas: Taylor Publishing Company, 1997.

Rosemond, J., *Ending the homework hassle.* Kansas City: Andrews McMeel, 1990.

Sells, S. *Treating the tough adolescent.* New York, NY: Guilford Press, 2004.

Severe, S., *How to behave so your children will, too.* New York: Viking Press, 2000.

Shapiro, J., "Therapy for Tough Kids and Their Beleaguered Families." A program sponsored by Cross Country University, San Antonio, TX September 9, 2005.

Spitzer, R., Davies, M., Barkley, R., "The DSM III-R field trials of disruptive behavior disorders." *Journal of the American Academic of Child and Adolescent Psychiatry* 1990; 29:690-697.

Sutton, J., *What parents need to know about ODD.* Pleasanton, TX: Friendly Oaks Publications, 2007 (text revision).

_____, *Current "best practice" strategies for managing oppositional defiant disorder.* (an audio of a program presented at Laurel Ridge Treatment Center, San Antonio, TX) Pleasanton, TX: Friendly Oaks Publications, 2003.

_____, *101 ways to make your classroom special: creating a place where significance, teamwork and spontaneity can sprout and flourish.* Pleasanton, TX: Friendly Oaks Publications, 1999.

_____, *If my kid's so nice ... why's he driving me crazy?* Pleasanton, TX: Friendly Oaks Publications, 1997.

_____, *It makes a difference.* Pleasanton, TX: Friendly Oaks Publications, 1990 (reprinted in 2002).

_____, *Passive aggressive features of oppositional disorder: effects of specific training on teacher attitudes toward these behaviors in students.* Doctoral dissertation: Brigham Young University, 1981.

Turecki, S. (with Tonner, L.), *The difficult child.* New York: Bantom Books, 1985.

Wenning, K., *Winning cooperation from your child.* New York: Jason Aronson, 1999.

Werry, J., "Attention deficit, conduct, oppositional, and anxiety disorders in children; a review of research in differentiating characteristics." *Journal of the American Academy of Child and Adolescent Psychiatry* 1987; 26;133-143.

Wong, H., Wong, R., *The first days of school: how to be an effective teacher.* California: Harry K. Wong Publications, 2004.

Quality Keynotes and Training for Educators

Presented by Dr. James Sutton

▓ Most Popular Keynotes

Don't Lose Your Marbles; Give 'Em Away!- This keynote urges participants to become encouragers of young people. The program has a history of successfully delivering a powerful message wrapped in humor and inspiration.

▓ Training Programs

Working Effectively with the Difficult, Defiant and Noncompliant Student- This program will take an intensive look at ways of working with the noncompliant and defiant student, focusing on behaviors of procrastination, pouting and stubbornness, obstructionism and forms of intentional inefficiency, such as "forgetting" and chronic episodes of missing or incomplete school work.

The Kid Who Doesn't Care- This program focuses on working with the socially-challenged student. Behaviors like fighting, lying, stealing and destruction of property will be covered, as well as interventions for more effectively managing this youngster.

Support Staff Training- Dr. Sutton also does training for counselors, social workers and school psychologists on topics relating to depression, anxiety, ODD, conducting a diagnostic interview and strategies for group counseling.

▓ About Dr. Sutton

■ Nationally recognized psychologist

■ Has taught everything from grade school to graduate school

■ Committed to platform excellence (*Certified Speaking Professional*)

■ Clients include 54 universities

■ Bestselling, award-winning author

▓ Add Value; Save Money

Ask about the ***Keynote with Breakout Package***

Breakout programs (about 2 hours) include:

When the Kid Who Can, WON'T- Dr. Sutton addresses the challenges of working with the capable, but difficult, student. Lots of take-away ideas.

The Angry Child-This program offers help and hope in reaching the volatile and aggressive child.

Addressing Oppositional & Defiant Behavior: Current "Best Practice" Strategies- A program for support staff (counselors, social workers, school psychologists, etc.).

Partial Client List:

Boysville
Brigham Young University
Cal Farley's Boys Ranch
Caring Family Network
Florida State University
Indiana University
Juvenile Justice Association of Michigan
Kentucky Association of Psychologists in the Schools
Louisiana State University
National Association of Children with Learning Disabilities
National Association of Homes for Children
New Mexico Children's Services
Oklahoma School Psychologists' Association
Pennsylvania School Counselors' Association
Penn State University
Syracuse University
Texas Association of School Psychologists
Texas Educational Diagnosticians' Assn
Texas Tech University
Universities of Alabama, Arizona, Kansas, Missouri, Nebraska, North Carolina, Oklahoma and Texas

---

For more information contact:

Dr. James D. Sutton
Pleasanton, Texas
www.DocSpeak.com

800-659-6628

What others have said:

No way to outclass Dr. Sutton. He holds his audience!
Bob Peterson, San Antonio, Texas

Given the quality of your presentations, I'm not at all surprised that you're in such high demand!
Dean **Charles Wilson**, PhD, Shreveport, Louisiana

Dr. Sutton was an awesome keynoter! He captivated the conference participants and most certainly touched every heart. I promise, you could have heard a pin drop during his entire presentation. It was amazing!
Debbie Buchanan, Edinburg, Texas

Books by
Dr. James Sutton

(for descriptions, go to **www.DocSpeak.com** and click on "Books and Resources," or run off the current newsletter on the website.)

(Substantial discounts are available to schools on quantity orders of *101 Ways to Make Your Classroom Special*)

Send, phone or fax order to:

Friendly Oaks Publications
PO Box 662, Pleasanton, TX 78064
(830) 569-3586 fax: (830) 281-2617

Order Form

(Quantity)	(Description)	(Amount)
_____	*101 Ways to Make Your Classroom Special ($11.95)*	_____
_____	*If My Kid's So Nice, Why's He Driving ME Crazy? ($18.95)*	_____
_____	*60 Ways to Reach a Difficult and Defiant Child ($21.50)*	_____
_____	*It Makes a Difference ($14.00)*	_____
_____	*Windows II ($21.50)*	_____
_____	*What Parents Need to Know About ODD ($21.95)*	_____
_____	***PACKAGE DISCOUNT:*** *All six books ($96.00)*	_____

Date:_____

8.25% Sales Tax (Texas only) _____

Shipping & Handling   _$4.50_

TOTAL: _____

Ship this order to:

Name:_____

Address:_____

City:_____

State/Zip:_____

Daytime Phone:_____

Order paid by (circle one): Check   Charge Card

_____ Visa   _____ MasterCard

Card #:_____

Expiration date:_____

Notes

Notes

Notes

Notes

Notes

Notes

Notes

Printed in the United States
88401LV00002B/515-754/A

9 781878 878748